Biblical Interpretations in Preaching

Biblical Interpretations in Preaching

Gerhard von Rad
Translated by John E. Steely

Abingdon   Nashville

BIBLICAL INTERPRETATIONS IN PREACHING

Originally published in 1973 as *Predigt-Meditationen*

Translation copyright © *1977 by Abingdon*

Translation from the German language with the approval of the Publishing House Vandenhoeck and Ruprecht, Göttingen. © Vandenhoeck & Ruprecht, Göttingen.

Library of Congress Cataloging in Publication Data

RAD, GERHARD von, 1901–1971.
  Biblical interpretations in preaching.
  Translation of Predigt-Meditationen.
  1. Lutheran Church—Sermons. 2. Sermons, German. 3. Bible—Homiletical use. I. Title.
BX8066.R22P7413   251   76-43248

ISBN 0-687-03444-2

Scripture quotations noted RSV are from the Revised Standard Version of the Bible, copyrighted 1946, 1952, © 1971, 1973.

MANUFACTURED BY THE PARTHENON PRESS AT
NASHVILLE, TENNESSEE, UNITED STATES OF AMERICA

Translator's Preface

The eminent author of this book long ago put students of the Bible in his debt by his scholarly works on the Old Testament. In the present work he shows how that scholarly labor is utilized in the task of proclaiming the word of God in the church.

My task thus has been rewarding for several reasons: it is a pleasure to share in offering Professor Gerhard von Rad's insights to a larger company of readers; I have been enriched personally as I have read these pages; and I welcome this persuasive demonstration of how scholarship can and does serve the life of the church, of how exegesis can and does enhance preaching.

These lines, composed at the end of the work of translating, are written in the awareness of my debt to my family for their help and encouragement. I should like also to thank the members of the Poteat Class at Pullen Memorial Baptist Church, who challenge me week by week to bring exegetical study to bear upon the questions of our individual and common life. Though the book itself is not mine to dedicate, I should like to dedicate my work in the translation to these friends. They will respond, as is their custom, with still more questions of their own.

John E. Steely
Wake Forest, North Carolina

Foreword

The homiletical meditations presented here appeared between 1946 and 1966 chiefly in the *Göttinger Predigtmeditationen* and are now published together at the suggestion of the publisher. The only text previously unpublished, the excursus on exegesis and preaching that is prefixed to the collection, requires a brief explanation.

In the winter semester of 1965/66 my father, together with Prof. Günther Bornkamm and Prof. Hans Freiherr von Campenhausen, established an exegetical-homiletical practicum for theological students, which he opened with an exposition of the fundamental connection between exegesis and preaching. The plan for this first seminar session was found written out in full among my father's manuscripts. Of course it was never intended for publication; rather, it quite unmistakably bears the marks of oral address and improvisation. These cannot be eliminated, even by abridgment or by polishing, without destroying the character of the whole. If the text was to be printed at all, it had to be printed just as it was, even though as a result several casually spoken expressions are given more weight than is actually their due. The text can be understood only in terms of the specific situation for which it was first written. It is related throughout to a very particular group of hearers and partners in dialogue; it does not offer any complete set of facts, but attempts to provide stimuli for the dialogue. Thus understood, it may appear suited after all to open this series of sermonic meditations.

Heidelberg, March 1973   Ursula von Rad

Contents

About
Exegesis and Preaching

We have announced this practicum because we are aware, just as you are, of the difficulties and questions which exist today between the two entities of exegesis and preaching and because there is something of a gap in our proposed course offerings. We shall not discuss here whether these difficulties are as new as many today believe, or whether every age has not had to suffer them in its own way. It is sufficient to say that the questions are there, and we propose to address ourselves to them.

There are two principles established for us; on these we three leaders of this practicum are in agreement.

1. The biblical texts *must* be preached—under all circumstances and at any cost. The people for whom we each have a responsibility need them for living (and for dying).

2. The biblical texts *can* be preached. This is a battleground, and there is much that must be clarified here. But if we did not have this firm conviction, this practicum would be meaningless, and we would not have announced it.

Thus on these points we three have agreed. Everything else is open. Now, to be sure, I should like to give you a warning: don't expect any exhibition matches here! You must share in the work—that is the *conditio sine qua non*. Protective aid, then, is readily assured to the person who takes a vulnerable position. But it will not do for you simply to let yourself be fed here. This means, specifically, that you must do preparatory work; you must come to the meetings of the practicum with an opinion already formed and take a stand.

So the business we are going to undertake here is that of *interpretation*. Both scientific exegesis and preaching are interpretation. Interpretation is always appropriation of an intellectual content that is being transmitted to us. No understanding at all is possible without some form of inward appropriation. It would be an illusion to think that we could deal with the transmitted intellectual contents as a foundry worker handles molten ore with long-handled ladles—and thus keep them at a distance from ourselves. Moreover, no understanding is possible unless what is to be interpreted is applied to ourselves, unless it touches us existentially. Therefore there is also no fundamental distinction between exegesis and preaching. Preaching, too, is interpretation, only in a different form of speech, in a different confrontation. Nevertheless we separate the two modes of work. So now first a word about exegesis and then a word about preaching.

When we come today to talk about exegesis, we must reckon rather universally with a blind spot, an often total incapacity for, and indeed even a lack of understanding of, the task that is involved and of what is to be undertaken here. Perhaps it would be helpful if we could go together and spend half an hour looking around in the exhibition "Ars Sacra" on medieval books and bookcraft. The impression that thrusts itself upon one there is this: look at how one can honor a book, celebrate it; see how unutterably painstaking one can be in copying, in ornamenting the initial letters, in creating illustrations; witness the toil in devotion, in submission—ah, simply this: just look how the book is received and affirmed here! And in the unbelievable precision of handwork—what vitality, indeed, even excitement! Unquestionably in any dealing with books the element of handwork is prominent, something that can be done cleanly or sloppily. In the "handwork" of interpretation, for example, what is involved includes knowledge and mastery of a foreign language and historical setting, concentration upon the substance, and respect for the word and the text, from which then grows a capacity for distinguishing this form of discourse and that. Let us assume that a project involves a matter of history; still there are so many ways possible for conjuring up the past! The saga does it in a way entirely different from, say, that of the Deuteronomic writer of history. And when prophets begin to treat history, to open history up to view in a prophetic manner, then the hearing and seeing of the positivist who insists on exact history disappears.

Large parts of the Bible are written in an elevated artistic language. What does this signify? Nothing, if we regard poetry as rhetorical finery. Much, when we consider that poetic discourse is a quite specific form of the recognition and expression of reality, with the reservation that it is not interchangeable with another form. When a geographical name appears, it must not remain a mere sound. Surprising perspectives will often open up through the use of such names.

Believe me, one does not so quickly make out the aim of a text or where it is leading—not even the well-known ones and those that apparently move into a religious jargon that is familiar to us. The greatest enemy of any orderly interpretation is the uncritical paraphrase, a simple repeating of the text with a few words changed. The *critical* paraphrase, of course, is the crown of any interpretation. One cannot possibly do better than voice in a few clean sentences the structure of meaning that has been comprehended. That is the paradoxical mystery of all good exposition: the more we at first keep ourselves in the background, the more we seek to approach the text with clean hands for our task, and the less we interrupt the text with our own questions, the more directly will the text address us. What finer moment than when such a text begins to speak, often quite differently from what was expected! But what does it do? It speaks. Do you not know the joy of exegesis? No, you do not! If you did, then why this current running after summary statements, after summaries of contents? The dullest abstract summary gets more recognition nowadays than the source itself. No wonder study makes people weary and discontent! And still another thing: how uninteresting, when one is engaged in this work, are the questions about theological tendencies! This interest in theological schools and tendencies is simply something for feebleminded folk!

Let me develop my ideas a bit further. Interpretation is always a translation. Indeed, every translation is itself an interpretation. Not a single word in the ancient language exactly coincides with the corresponding word in our language. Language and mind are a unity. We cannot translate as though Isaiah or John spoke German. That would be anything but a faithful translation. Something of that which could actually be said only in Hebrew or Greek must be taken up into the translation. This foreignness must not be lost in a smooth, flowing German text. Thus in a good translation one must activate and employ every conceivable possibility that our language affords, in order to confront the foreign element that one finds. Full correspondence is never to be achieved.

One special problem is the rapid decline in language that is occurring among us. Many are not even aware that they are employing only narrow, worn-out cliches, with which they cannot get at the immense breadth and the wealth of nuances of the biblical vocabulary. Schleiermacher once very pointedly stated the problem of translation: "Either the translator leaves the author resting peacefully insofar as possible and brings the reader to him; or he leaves the reader resting peacefully insofar as possible and brings the author to him" (Schleiermacher, *Sämtliche Werke*, III, 2, 207 ff.). The former is the way of scientific exegesis, and the latter is that of preaching (even though not in such a fashion that the hearer is left untroubled by the text!).

This brings us to the second point—preaching. Allow me to make a little side trip into a nontheological area. In the period from 1900 to 1914 something of great significance happened in German poetry. Many poets found themselves increasingly unable to express the realities they perceived in the language that had come down to them, the language of Goethe and the Romantics. Goethe, the Romantics, and the Later Romantics (active even to the present) had an intellectual world, a supporting system of values, into which they fitted their poems as into a broad panoramic view. These traditional concepts, value judgments, and poetic forms would no longer hold up; and over against them arose an entirely new experience of the world. The previously banal, poetically irrelevant, and neutral set in motion something immense, unfathomable. (Here I can only describe the phenomenon, not the reasons for it, for the latter would take us into a boundless region.) Thus the fact is that the poetic art of that time (and poetry, too, strives for precision in its utterances) in its leading representatives felt itself to have been left desolate by the previous and prevailing possibilities of expression; these had become strangely empty, mechanical, or at any rate utterly unsuited for articulating the reality with which these poets felt themselves overwhelmingly confronted. For what would result from the reality which they could no longer articulate in language! All these poets sensed their dilemma as something frightful. Hofmannsthal, who very early and perhaps most clearly expressed (in his *Chandos-*

15

brief) the experience of the decay of language and of fearful doubt in the face of the world, did not succeed in overcoming this crisis. He continued to write poetry but did not himself break any more new ground. He speaks of the "decorum of silence" that remained. Others were able to save themselves only by attempting to gain apperception of the newly experienced reality in entirely new ways, often in great ventures, in experiments in language.

We are not directly concerned here with this monstrous phenomenon (it also affected painters and musicians). The preacher is not a poet. The matter which he has to put in language is different. The poets thus cannot help him in his business. But we are indirectly concerned with the poets' dilemma. The pastor must know about it. The people to whom he addresses himself (particularly the young people) are more and more being sucked into this doubt about the world. Among other things, this means that the preacher must do away with all pseudopoetic ornamentation. Otherwise he exposes his own cause to a devastating suspicion. With both the intellectuals and the laborers he loses the ground which perhaps he still can hold with the bourgeois congregation. But that is not all. In the area of the Christian vocabulary, in fact, we have experienced a very similar process of disintegration and emptying of our traditional Christian language. Bonhoeffer said that in repeating the great biblical themes we would have to begin at the very beginning. My fellow students, what real progress it would be should a part of the common property of our theology become the awareness that the Bible with its language (languages!) far transcends the capacity of expression of our contemporary language. To sound the theological alarm today, more than sixty years after the *Chandosbrief,* would be ridiculous. The task to which we have to do justice has been known and recognized for a

16

long time: we must reproduce the utterance of the Bible in our language just as concretely (just as concretely *ad hominem*) as it was meant in the Bible. Going off into unnecessary religious generalities is one of the greatest sins in preaching. And it is worth nothing at all to switch into clever jargon in order to appear up-to-date.

There is in fact a fundamental difference between ourselves and the poets I have spoken of. The world to which they have to give expression in dread and delight does not speak (not in words at any rate); its mystery must be coaxed from it with the most daring experiments. We are commissioned to reproduce the words of speaking persons. And here I want only to suggest something that is quite presumptuous. It could be that Christians could make a helpful contribution, through their knowledge of God and the world, to the problem with which our poets are grappling. We would have to convince them that both world and man can be understood and can survive only in relation to God.

The great discovery which all of you must make in preaching is that the texts themselves actually speak (Deutero-Isaiah must have experienced something like a panting and groaning on God's part when he was silent for a while! [Isa. 42:14]). The best sermons are those in which one notes the preacher's own surprise that—and how—the text suddenly began to speak. I have heard sermons in which one had the feeling that the preacher only stepped a little to one side in order to let the text speak (now of course he had already done something more!). In the *Kirchenkampf* [the German church's struggle with the Nazi regime] I heard sermons in which the text slipped out of the preacher's hands and fell from the pulpit; it was so incredibly timely and pertinent that the preacher completely lost control over it. These may be extreme cases, but they are still better than trite, hackneyed Christian chatter. Good sermons have something of an intellectual adventure about them. I give you about ten to twenty beginners' sermons, in which you will repeat what you have learned. Then you will have preached yourselves out. Then if you do not make the discovery that every text wants to speak for itself, you are lost. We are dealing with that word that is sharper than a two-edged sword.

> O God, we lift our prayer to thee,
> Thou gracious, generous Lord,
> That thou wilt grant us power to live
> As children true to thee.
> Send us thy word divine,
> That sharp two-edged sword
> To arm us for the fight
> Against the gates of hell.

Now since I am quoting from a hymnbook, I will say one further word in conclusion. It is a churchly business that we are pursuing. The way many young theologues are dissociating themselves from the church is highly displeasing to me. It is also utterly unrealistic. Many do not attend church at all any more, but then they will expect a brisk church attendance when they preach! When we say "church," we also mean the duly constituted church. Certainly many will have much on their minds by way of criticism of our church government. But it still is true that we delegate the less pleasant tasks to a church government which in the last analysis requires our participation and collaboration. Criticism of the established church does not become credible and creditable until the critic also, and even more so, sweeps the walk in front of his own doorway.

With this, let our work begin. I hope that now you, too, where it appears to you to be needed, will boldly have your own say. "I have made my first speech, dear Theophilus."

Genesis 4:1-16

Invocavit

The story of Cain and Abel tells simply about man. It must once have been an etiological tribal saga, but now, as its position in the great preface to the Yahwist's primeval history shows, it is expanded into something pertaining to all humanity and primeval history in general. (The meaning of the etymology of the name given in verse 1b is obscure.)

Mankind now is divided into different estates, with diverse manners of life. But this cultural diversity goes very deep: the two altars are its most disturbing sign. The narrator sees nothing strange in the fact that both Cain and Abel offer sacrifices. In fact, he even regards it as obvious that each man would present the best of his worldly goods as a sign that he views God as the true owner of all that he possesses. The narrator in no way explains why God did not "regard" Cain's sacrifice. We must warn against psychologizing here; the reason hardly lay in Cain's attitude and probably did not lay in the area of ritual (unless it is that Abel's sacrifice was accepted because it was a bloody sacrifice). The reason for the decision in Abel's favor is—contrary to most traditional interpretations!—to be found entirely in the freedom of the divine grace. This decision cannot be tested in terms of human logic, but the principle stated in Exodus 33:19b does apply to it. On the other hand, it should be remembered that the decision does not mean that Cain is cast into the pit of hell, as indeed is shown in God's gracious address that follows. Nevertheless God did not accept this sacrifice. Hot resentment rises up in Cain at this; evil begins to affect man even in physical aspects. Cain envies Abel the friendly countenance of God (Zimmerli, 1. *Mose 1-11*, I, 268). Abel is killed because of God. If even the immanent struggle in competition is a bitter one, the conflict, which in the last analysis concerns the existence of God, is utterly terrible. The struggles of churches and world views of recent years have once again given us an intimation of this fact. "In politica ira est aliquid humani reliquum. . . . talis furia in politica ira non est. . . . furor pharisaicus est furor plane diabolicus" (Luther, *Werke*, Weimar edition, XLII, 193).

In the words of verse 7 (divine pastoral care!) God is able to refer to an agreement in relation to Cain ("Is it not true . . . ?"). The difficult $s^e eth$, "lift up," probably is to be connected with the downcast countenance; "you can lift it up," i.e., "freely look up." Sin appears here as an objective power that is located outside man, one that seizes possessions as a robber does. Yet Cain is charged with full responsibility for sin. As in the case of the first sin, in the Fall, the murder immediately brings God onto the scene. But whereas in that former case the question was "Where art thou?" in the latter case Cain is asked about his brother ("The question of God now is posed as a social question" [Vischer, *Jahwe der Gott Kains*, p. 45]). Thus Cain was still graciously given the opportunity to respond with a confession (Zimmerli, in *ibid.*, p. 273), but Cain disposes of this most difficult of God's questions with a cynical witticism: "Am I supposed to look after the shepherd?"

Thus far the picture of the man is drawn—though at first still somewhat as foreground. But now the narrative opens up dimensions which Cain had not taken into account. The blood of the murdered man raises its accusing cry to the throne of God ($s^e ak$ is exactly the same as was understood in old German law by the term *Zeterruf*, the appeal for legal protection [cf. II Kings 8:3; Deut. 22:24, 27]). And God is the protector of all rights. All life belongs to him—an extremely important principle of Old Testament belief (Gen. 9:6; Ps.

24:1). Cain has trespassed on God's rights of eminence and property! And besides that, something horrible has happened, something that can never be made right. Ancient man sensed it much more clearly than do we: the earth, intended by God to serve man as the maternal foundation of life itself, has drunk a brother's blood! Here the punishment begins: the solidarity between man and earth is hopelessly shattered (the first disturbance of the relationship has already been seen in Gen. 3:17-18). Man now has forfeited the God-given right to a homeland on the earth (today even the quietest rural community knows about this fugitive and wanderer status). The preacher should present this fact and in addition should deliver the message from God that is committed to him for that purpose, especially since the narrative itself in fact has an explicit etiological focus: whence the homelessness of Cain? But bound up with this curse is something still more dreadful. A settled, established existence, a home on the earth before the "face of God" is for our narrator equivalent to the state of salvation. If Cain has lost his right to a home on the earth and is cursed by God, therewith he has lost God, God's nearness, and above all God's protection; hence Cain's cry (vs. 13), which is not to be interpreted as an expression of a readiness to repent or of a dreadful awareness of guilt. *Awon* is to be translated here as "punishment." Cain immediately surveys it: What lies ahead of him is utterly unendurable, for a life without God is a life which God no longer protects. Man today must also painfully relearn this fact. Indeed, Cain knows full well the law that spilled blood must bring forth a continuing harvest of evil.

But at its conclusion the story points to a great mystery. It is not Cain but God who has the last word. If it is an enigma as to why Cain was not slain because he had committed murder, it is utterly amazing that Cain, the man under a curse from God, yet is taken by God into a wholly

21

paradoxical protective relationship. The sign—in an earlier form of the story the idea probably meant a kind of tattoo—is to be understood as a mark of protection. Even when Cain goes out from before the face of God he still remains God's possession. God's right of lordship over Cain miraculously is not abolished. It is not God's will that the punishment which he imposed upon Cain should give man the right to turn savage and to shed blood. So the story of Cain ends with a restrained word of a divine intention of grace and order.

At the beginning of Passiontide it is fitting to say a word about the extent of the damage done by man. Man approaching the cross is a brother-murderer from the very beginning. The interpreter may also properly sketch out the lines of cultural history—the division of humanity into various states of life, the existence of two altars. And Cain continues to travel the road he has taken—founding cities and the musical arts, developing the art of forging so that the sword comes to be regarded as an approved implement—and the song of Lamech madly celebrates the native force and the boundlessness of revenge (Gen. 4:17-24).

But the sermon should center on verse 10: as far as human understanding is concerned, inconceivable and inexpiable is the accusing cry of the blood of our brother Abel, a cry that ascends to God day and night. This should be the starting point for the dispelling of manifold and familiar misunderstandings: Abel's blood, even the best and dearest, never brings salvation in the presence of God; instead it increases the burden of the curse. But Christ's blood "speaks more graciously than the blood of Abel" (Heb. 12:24). Thus the Bible speaks of two kinds of blood and their voices before God: one of these is millionfold, and its message is accusation, while the other is the blood of the One, and it brings healing. An *Invocavit*

22

sermon on Genesis 4 may—as from a great distance—point to the cross of Christ.

Genesis 12:1-9

For any exposition of the Yahwist's pericope of Abraham's migration an awareness of its close connection with the preceding primeval history is utterly crucial. This primeval narrative had set forth a history of God's dealing with the world and with men. The Fall, Cain's murder of his brother, Lamech's wild song of vengeance, angelic marriages, the building of the Tower of Babel—with these stages a constantly widening breach was pictured. And at the end of this road stood God's judgment upon humanity—its division into peoples who no longer understand each other and are now scattered over the whole earth. Yet this primeval history displays still another, less evident, line: in spite of the threat of immediate death, God did not let the first men die. In fact, in an act of mercy he clothed them for their departure from Paradise. Cain was placed under a curse, to be sure; yet he was kept by God in an utterly paradoxical protective relationship. The story of the flood came forth as an assurance of divine patience and of a divine will to order. Thus God's judging rule also again and again displayed, as its inner side or its extension, a concealed saving intention. But the end of the story of the Tower of Babel shows a judgment without mercy. Was that God's final word on humanity? (One could say that the primeval history is aimed at making this question urgent for the reader.) Here the salvation history begins, with the story of Abraham. The transition certainly is very abrupt:

up to this point we read about universal things, about the world, humanity, woman, sin, suffering, the nations; now the scene is narrowed, and one individual man stands in the reader's field of vision. But in its very beginning this incipient salvation history gives the answer that in the primeval history had remained in doubt—that in Abraham all races on the earth were to be blessed! Here is given the etiology of all Israel's etiologies, and the bridging of the gulf between God and humanity as a whole is prophesied as the distant goal of God's abandonment. Thus the verses Genesis 12:1-3 are quite properly to be understood as the conclusion of the primeval history toward which the biblical narrator has been pressing or, at any rate, as the dovetailing of primeval history and salvation history.

God's call demands (with increasing urgency!) detachment from very strong ties—from the land (that is, the homeland), as well as from kinship and the family. But the man with the childless wife (Gen. 11:30) is to become a great nation. The great "name" which God will give certainly is to be understood in connection with Gen. 11:4: God intends to bestow fame after he has brought to nought the self-proclaimed fame of mankind. Indeed, now he introduces his salvation and judgment into history in such a way that, in the last analysis, blessing and curse will be determined by the position which people will take with respect to Abraham and his seed! (Evidently this is not to be determined—at any rate not explicitly—by what Abraham and his seed will say but by Abraham, that is, simply by Abraham's very existence.) The *wahyeh berakah* in 12:2b ("Be thou a blessing") could even mean that Abraham is to become a formula of blessing with which men in the future will wish blessings upon each other. But in no case can the meaning of *nibreku beka* ("With thee, in thee, shall they bless themselves") in 12:3 be taken to mean only that Abraham's abundance of blessings will become proverbial

24

among all the races of the earth, for this would be to dissolve the obvious connection of our pericope with the primeval history.

So Abraham sets out on this journey. The narrator dismisses as unimportant all that could have gone on in Abraham's soul; but he portrays the fact of Abraham's mute obedience in monumental simplicity, which precisely thus does justice to the whole scale and scope of the event (vss. 4-5). With this emigration begins Abraham's great alien existence and that of his seed, and the sermon should under no circumstances conceal what happens now in the following verses (6-9). The narrative began with a great outpouring of divine promises, but it does not go on to display a great and actually achievable goal or a tangible fulfillment. What great thing did Abraham find in Shechem and then later in the Negeb? And at the end of this road—in our text alone mention is made three times of departure and migration!—there will yet be nothing grand for Abraham, only a grave in the cave of Machpelah (and, in fact, not yet visible here by a long way is the lowest point to which this existence as an alien will lead, the night of God-forsakenness of Gethsemane and Golgotha). In any case the congregation's attention should be drawn to how our text, after its portentous beginning, comes to its close almost in meaninglessness. For according to the law by which Abraham went his way, that of his seed would turn out the same way. Of this seed of Abraham Luther says, in commenting on this passage: "In this same way they live in the world at all times; they are engaged in civic and social affairs; they guide states and establish families; they cultivate fields; they conduct business or practice hand-crafts; and yet they know that like their fathers they are aliens and temporary residents. In other words, they use the world as a temporary shelter which they must shortly leave . . . so that with the left hand, so to speak, they tend earthly

25

matters; but the right hand they lift up to the eternal homeland."

Earlier interpreters thought that even Abraham's taking Lot with him was actually contrary to God's intention; but it is more likely that the note in verse 5 is meant only to prepare the way for what is to be told in chapters 13 and 19.

The clause stating that the Canaanites dwelt in the land at that time (vs. 6b) could be an explanatory addition, but it is significant enough: Abraham by no means finds a vacant territory awaiting him, one which would at once become his own. Instead, he is brought into an existence (not at all adequately explained) alongside and in the midst of a pagan population, to which his relationship will be throughout that of an interloper and even an inferior. How many difficult issues lie hidden in this association!

But in this extremely problematical situation God comes to him with a new word of promise: the very land in which he now finds himself is to belong to his descendants. It will not belong to him; he will acquire as his own property only a very small bit of this land, his burial place (chap. 23); and thus he will be able to share in the promised gift only in dying. Is he not bound to wonder, as Calvin thinks, whether this *nudum verbum* ("bare word") is being uttered as a joke (*se haberi ludibrio*)? But now with verse 7 the promised gift is mentioned which in all the patriarchal narratives is the most important and indeed is almost equated with the blessing of salvation, the land of Canaan. If the preacher does not simply avoid this as embarrassing to himself and his hearers, he is confronted with the question of whether the old typological interpretation is not right after all. That interpretation held that corresponding to this Old Testament blessing of salvation in the New Testament is the new Christ-life that is promised to the believer, a life that is now hidden with Christ and will only be made manifest in the eschaton (Col. 3:3). It is striking also to note how the reception of the promise is temporally distributed over several separate experiences of perceiving the revelation. The most important revelation is the last to be perceived by Abraham.

At Shechem, also, Abraham erects an outwardly visible sign of his faith and builds an altar. Calvin comments on this point that the purely inward worship did not suffice: *"Non sufficere interiorem cordis cultum, nisi accedat externa apud homines professio"*—without the addition of an outward profession before men. This altar, erected not far from the heathen oracle-terebinth tree, was a sign (at first only a mute one) of immeasurable significance in relation to paganism. But there once again Abraham pulled up stakes and went farther and farther toward the south country (*halok wenaso*[a], "walking and departing"), "spreading the aroma of his faith" (Calvin).

In this story, in this Abraham who is uprooted, who has become an alien, who surrenders himself blindly to God and his leading, the church in all ages has seen the figure of faith and the way of faith set forth in a paradigm (*"communis typus vitae omnium fidelium,"*—"a type of the life that is common to all the faithful"—thus Calvin). Yet there is still one thing more to observe. All the more recent practical interpretations apply the contents of the pericope in an edifying way to the private and inward life of faith of the individual. Such an exclusively individualist handling of the text then of course can do justice neither to the so important linking of our pericope with the primeval history (see above) nor to the divine commitment in verse 3a,b. Now there is no doubt that in reading this ancient story ancient Israel recognized itself in Abraham as believing community, as people of God (and not primarily as individuals). The patriarchal narratives, which indeed apparently set forth such wholly personal fates and experiences of divine guidance, all have, to a lesser or

27

greater degree, that fine transparency for adaptation to what is collective and communal, in that they do express, above all, God's plans and directions for his people. In this sense these stories unquestionably function as types, without thereby losing the thrust of that which is unique in salvation history. Now it is true that there are for the church no great calls, or cases of divine guidance, trials, or divine assistance through trouble that are not at the same time call, guidance, trials, and divine assistance for the individual believer; and in this fact (but only therein!) lies also the right of that personal and individual interpretation and application of our text.

Genesis 16:1-16

Almost all the Abraham narratives are thematically characterized by the enigma of the delay in fulfillment of the promise. The Yahwistic and Elohistic pericopes set forth with great vividness the attacks and unusual conflicts into which the recipient of the promise is led by this delay. Thus even verse 1 of our story describes the difficulty of the situation which now because of a natural hindrance contains, in addition, something of an enigma: Sarah is barren; so by human calculations the heir of promise cannot be born of her at all. This fact now sets in motion some extremely dubious activity on the part of the participants.

To understand the unusual goings-on in Abraham's household, we must take into account legal usages which apparently were common in the ancient Orient and which the Code of Hammurabi also regulated. If in the case of childlessness the mistress gave a maidservant to her husband, the child thus born to the servant was regarded as the child of the wife; it was born "on her knees" (Gen. 30:3) and thereby became her child by adoption. Thus from the standpoint of the law and of the outlook of that time, Sarah's offer was entirely unobjectionable.

But certainly the narrator had his own ideas about how assistance was given here from the human side for the fulfillment of the divine promise—even if that assistance was supposed to have been offered by Sarah in "heroic self-denial" (Lange).

And now everything happens that we might expect, once the way of human self-assertiveness is taken. Hagar has no idea of renouncing the blessing of her womb in favor of her mistress. "Regard for nature arises powerfully and splendidly in Hagar" (Procksch). The fact that in the disagreement Sarah—who believed that she was entirely innocent in the matter!—turns not to Hagar but to Abraham is in keeping with the legal situation. Abraham gives way again; by giving Hagar back to Sarah he restores the old legal situation ("Abraham plays a somewhat unhappy role between these two strong-willed women" [Gunkel]). Hagar is driven by Sarah to extremities; she flees into the desert. Does she have hopes of being able to reach her old home in the South? This is how desperate things have become. But, above all, what becomes of Abraham's child? Is it after all the legacy of the promise?

God pursued Hagar. It is to be assumed that Hagar only gradually came to recognize the angel of the Lord as a divine being, for the Old Testament emissaries of God— they are not to be thought of as having wings—originally were regarded by men and women as being like themselves. But the "angel of Yahweh" is not some sort of heavenly being. The noteworthy thing is that no longer is a clear distinction at all made between Yahweh and him.

29

Again and again God speaks through the angel in direct discourse. He is apparently an earthly manifestation of God himself. We must also keep in mind that wherever the angel of the Lord appears in the Old Testament, it is to help, to defend, or to save; and he can be addressed directly as the covenant grace that has become a person. Thus we can understand how the ancient interpreters saw in him certain christological features.

The angel's two questions to Hagar (vs. 8), who is about to run away to her death, as well as her child's death, are of great importance. (Could they not provide the thrust for a sermon?) The consolation that he offers is also twofold. It is hortatory: Hagar must return and submit (vs. 9). And it is promising: Hagar will become the matriarch of a great people—wild, combative, and ardent in battle, all against all—a worthy offspring of its defiant mother. Here the narrative betrays its earlier etiological aim. It was once meant to explain the origin of the Bedouin tribe of the Ishmaelites; at any rate, the story dwells, not without sympathy, on this nomadic, aristocratic company of men who do not bow their necks to any yoke (the Old Testament speaks with admiration of the wild ass [Job 39:5-8]).

The appellations with which Hagar seeks to preserve the recollection of these divine epiphanies are very obscure. In verse 13 it is not clear whether she means the God who sees all or the God who discloses himself, who makes himself visible in the human sphere. Verse 13b is practically untranslatable ("Have I even here seen from behind the one who sees me?"). Are we to think here of Exodus 33:23? Obviously the narrator found in the old tradition some place names and etymologies which were already quite obscure and whose meaning he now abandons to the play of profound intellectual variations.

For its material the Hagar story reaches back into very remote times, as is shown by the complicated combination of a place etiology with a tribe etiology. In its present context, in which the significance of the etiologies obviously recedes, it must be interpreted in terms of the overarching theme of Abraham's receiving the promise and the delay in the fulfillment of this promise. And in this present context the story sets forth an extremely complicated situation that has arisen because the recipients of the promise could not wait and thus took matters into their own hands. "Thus the dark chain of Sarai's and Abram's disobedience twines around Hagar's pride, Sarai's hatred, Abram's indulgence, and Sarai's cruelty up to the point of Hagar's flight. It is as though—once the way of faith is abandoned and the way of human calculation is entered upon—man is snatched from the autonomy of obscurity and caught up in the unrolling of an iron chain of cause and effect" (Frey).

However, the preacher must stop in good time and guard against making the story into an allegory. Abraham and Sarah are not to be identified with the church and Hagar with the "natural man." (Nevertheless, in considering Hagar, who flees from Abraham's house into hopelessness, one can hardly avoid thinking of modern men and their future.) Not least of all, the several special historical and local traditions (which must not be evaporated by exegesis!) show that there is something unique in salvation history inherent in this event. And yet the interpreter may also see in Hagar's experience an occurrence that has typical significance. He may show in her how both striving to go beyond full trust and abandonment of patient waiting will lead one into situations and along ways where justice and injustice on the one hand and natural impulses on the other are hopelessly entangled. Such a path, then, when God's grace crosses it, will not be devoid of blessing, but it is not the way of salvation (Gen. 17:20-21); it leads to the battle of all against all. Indeed, the blessing of Ishmael is

31

only a shadow of the real Abrahamic blessing (cf. the quite similar parallel in Gen. 27:39-40), and yet it is a great marvel that God mercifully keeps his eyes open and watchful over that part of humanity in the desert and plants oases for them there (thus: "O thou God of blessing!"—vs. 13 according to Delitzsch). As this holds true primarily for the ways of God on a large scale and for those who depart from these ways, should it not also hold true in minor matters and personal issues? Everywhere the man called of God tends to follow the forbidden calculation of Sarah and the proud way of Hagar. In the sense of our story's context, on the other hand, man should be directed to nothing but a simple waiting on God.

In connection with this passage, earlier interpreters and preachers spoke quite naturally of very concrete domestic and personal issues—of the relationship of husband and wife, of guilt between spouses, of proper and improper indulgence, of the relationship to servants, and so forth. Why should not this area be open once again to us too? If we were only entirely sure that in this respect we were actually dealing with matters of the gospel and not moralizing! There can be no doubt that the story in no way intends to provide us with examples. The question as to which of the three persons has the fullest sympathy of the narrator is actually an idle question. The sermon must be careful, in the crucial matter, to treat not of human affairs, but of God's gracious ways of dealing with men.

Genesis 22:1-19

The story of Abraham's sacrificial journey is the most nearly perfect in form and the most inscrutable of all the patriarchal narratives. It is set forth by one "who has felt the horror in every fiber of his being" (Hirsch). Only a person who is completely out of step with the modest reserve of such a narrative can be misled in this regard. The connection of this passage with the preceding one is quite loose ("After these things"), and one may see here that our story once stood alone and had its meaning entirely within itself. We must now concern ourselves with interpreting it as a part of the entire context of the Abraham stories. Especially urgent is the task of securing the understanding of verse 1 against an interpretation that is widely offered nowadays in various versions. In that interpretation people take their point of departure in some respect from the general history of religions and speculate that the child sacrifice widely practiced by the heathen had become a temptation for Abraham (Israel). If the heathen offer to their gods what is dearest to them, can the call from Yahweh consist in his demanding any less of Israel? Then the narrative should be evaluated as documentation of "a humanizing and ethicizing" tendency (Hirsch). According to this view Israel in Genesis 22 has given an accounting of what Yahweh requires and what he does not require. Now we may leave undecided the question of whether the strict believer in the Yahweh of the old covenant actually would have let himself be so strongly impressed by the Canaanite practice of child sacrifice. A decisive argument against this interpretation is the fact that in that covenant the demand upon Abraham is explicitly made by God. The word "God" is especially emphasized by the syntax (it is placed before the verb!). Thus the explanation of child sacrifice as an adoption from the Canaanites is untenable, even in the restricted and tortuous form "that through the wicked tradition of human sacrifice in the Near East the divine command became for Abraham a misapprehension, although a providentially fateful and ultimately salutary misapprehension" (Lange).

But now a scientific analysis of our text appears to concede the correctness of that religiohistorical interpretation. At any rate there can be no doubt that in its earlier form the story was a *hieros logos*, an etiological cult saga, which provided the sacral legitimation for the replacement of human (or child) sacrifice by an animal sacrifice. Through a special divine revelation, this place was consecrated as a cultic place; and here the deity deigned to accept the life of an animal instead of that of a human. Something like this was the meaning of the narrative in a very much earlier form than its present one. But what was that cultic place? The name of the place involved—it is indeed anything but inconsequential!—is always of the greatest significance in the cult sagas. Its absence in Genesis 22 is a sure sign that in the present form the entire etiological train of ideas no longer plays a part; it has died out. We can see how the narrative plays with the etymology of the name (vs. 14), but the name itself, with the atrophy of the ancient etiological scope, has disappeared. Thus one must reckon with a very profound transformation of the entire intellectual and spiritual structure of meaning of the ancient narrative, for it is obvious that already in the time of the Elohist the readers no longer read the story as a cult legend of an old Israelite holy place.

And yet there can be no doubt that the new meaning which now illumines the old structure of the narrative can be grasped only in close connection with the larger context of the preceding history of Abraham. It is only thus that we open up the way to a proper interpretation of Genesis 22, and it may now have become clear that any discussion of the practice of child sacrifice should be kept out of the sermon.

34

It is much more appropriate to speak of the obligation of radical obedience. There is already something of Matthew 10:37-38 in this call of God to Abraham, and Hirsch has correctly seen that over against this total divine sovereign right, anything Promethean on man's side is totally lacking. And yet under no circumstances may we stop with this thought, for this would very seriously misplace the import of the passage. The child Isaac is not, as is commonly said in the language of ethics, just "the material of the obligation" in which Abraham's obedience had to be confirmed. Isaac is the gift of promise; contained in him is all the blessing which God had promised to give to Abraham. Thus it is by no means only a case of something natural, even though the story has to do with the offering of an only son; instead, it is a matter of questioning every reassuring content of faith, or at any rate a *certamen spirituale* (Calvin: a "spiritual struggle"), that is, God's conflict with his own promise. So, unfortunately, we can only say, in response to all the plaintive reflections concerning the harshness of history that are offered by a Christian humanism, that history involves much more frightful events than the sacrifice of a child. Luther, in his expositions, frequently stresses the extraordinary and exceptional aspect of these trials and sees them as far more grievous than the assaults that arise from the flesh or issue from the devil. They are the ones that come only to the *summi ex sanctis*, the "chief of the saints"; they are *vere patriarchales tentationes, quae posteri non potuissent ferre* ("truly patriarchal afflictions, which their successors would not have been able to bear"). Abraham's journey to Moriah can be viewed only *seu ex longinquo* ("as from a distance"), and Luther confesses of himself: *"Ego non potuissem esse spectator neque actor et mactator"* ("I could not have been a spectator, let alone a participant or the executioner"), and he very drastically compares us, persons

35

not directly involved, with the asses that were left at the foot of the mountain. Thus, we continue to insist, what is involved here is more than a child; it has to do with the promise, the sole divine consolation in life and in death. If Isaac's birth was already a matter for laughter (Gen. 18:12; 17:17; 21:6), what kind of laughter would await Abraham when he returned from sacrificing his child!

Thus on the one hand the sermon would have the task of communicating to the congregation something of the uniqueness of this event, the absence of any analogy to it, the fact that something is offered there that we cannot simply imitate—which is to say, that in this instance the way Abraham travels leads to a Godforsakenness which first was fully borne by Christ on the night when he was betrayed. On the other hand, to be sure, it may not be difficult to show how the life of all those who are baptized into Christ's death at least stands under the sign of that continuing surrender of the promise. If the sun of divine grace is darkened, if God's nearness, comfort, assurance, and hope vanish from our sight (like Isaac in Abraham's case), then we are to know that in such severe trials God is testing our faith. But only God can put an end to such trials. Calvin warns that no one should demand his own release prematurely *("Ne sibi quisque missionem ante tempus postulet")*, and Luther engages in some thoughts, indeed not idle thoughts, about how Abraham could have recognized the call in verses 11-12 as actually coming from God and not from the devil.

Now, as important as the clarification of the theological content of our chapter is (and we shall continue with this task in a moment), still this work may in no case lead to the result that the preacher, in a hypertheological spiritualizing, lays aside, like a husk, the unique narrative in which this content is given to us. In this case it is offered to the community in the event of Genesis 22, and this community

36

has the obligation and the right to hear it in just this form and to remember it thus. Of course, in view of the decidedly modest forbearance on the part of the narrator, tending toward moderation of feeling (which indeed leaves all sorts of room for imagination!), a warning must be given against any dramatic embellishment. "It is an astounding thing . . . and I readily confess that I am unable to follow these ideas and feelings, either with words or in thought" (Luther). Yet one word should be said about the portrayal of the journey. In apportioning the burdens, the father took upon himself the dangerous items: the knife and the container for the fire. "And the two of them walked together" (vs. 6). And then the conversation! "It would be a hopeless task for any of the greatest poets in world literature, from Aeschylus to Shakespeare and Goethe to imagine what Abraham and Isaac [said] to each other as they were walking together to the place where the father would sacrifice the son. Here the simplest and absolute solution . . ." (Steinthal). The father's answer to the child's question is indeed one of "love that intends to spare the beloved any pain" but not one of "an intimation of hope" (Delitzsch). Along with the submission to God's will which it expresses, Abraham's response is marked by a remarkable ambiguity, of which Abraham himself, of course, is not conscious. It is one of those answers "such as are only *given*" (Frey). "And the two of them walked together" (vs. 0). Nowhere else does the Old Testament mention a "land of Moriah" (the ancient translators reproduce the word differently, so it is doubtful whether the ancient narrator was thinking of the location of the later temple [II Chron. 3:1]). The preparations for the sacrifice are pictured in dreadful detail. At the last, the narrator's pace slows almost to a halt ("he stretched out his hand . . . took the knife"). Again it is the angel of Yahweh who intervenes to save (see above on Gen. 16). What God says in verses 15 and following confirms to Abraham in

37

superabundant fashion precisely what for him had just been made entirely uncertain. "The absence of any joyful utterance is part of the ancient grandeur of the passage, which shows no trace of sentimental features" (Procksch). According to a late Jewish tradition, after the two returned home Sarah uttered six cries and then died.

Now once again the question as to the aim of the story. We have already seen that the ancient intention, which was to explain the origin of the cult, had already been lost by the time of the Elohist. It now has to do with something more spiritual than the legitimacy of a cultic place. In view of the question which is raised by this fact, the interpreter cannot adequately guard against the insertion of some sort of "universal religious truths" ("God wills life," etc.; cf. the poem by Uhland "Ver sacrum") or even against "the mysterious truth . . . that in the relationship with God, the issues are always those of life and death" (Hirsch). Instead, we have seen that the story simply has to do with the *gift of promise* and, in this context, with the establishing of a *test* aimed at demonstrating true *fear of God* (vs. 12). In the first place, one must hold to these three basic ideas. Thus here it apparently is a matter of the exercise of obedience in an extreme case, specifically, of obedience toward a God who, it seems, intends to retract his promise. But God does not cancel that promise. This possibility is ruled out from the start, i.e., in the very first sentence of our story. It was the one temptation, a testing, to be sure, of a very special kind: Abraham is confronted with the question of whether he actually understands the promise as a pure gift of God and thus as something to which he has no legal right, no human claim. The story gives confirmation of the absolute gift character of the promise (similarly Gen. 48:8-14). God wills that none of his gifts should become for us an assured possession, least of all the gifts of his promise.

Still another implication immediately follows from this

38

reflection: once Isaac was thus placed on the altar and given back to God, he remains God's possession in a very special sense. In Isaac the community saw itself represented; in Isaac it saw itself offered up to God; in Isaac it confessedly had received back from God's hand its entire existence and now knew itself to be living solely by his grace and entrusted to his will. At the beginning we saw that the understanding of our narrative had of course to begin with the acknowledgment of the supreme divine rights over the life and death of man; in the same way now, at the end of our meditation, this radical divine claim is shown in a new form—precisely the one of Isaac, who was offered to God but given back "to life" and now is wholly subject to the will of the one who in the freedom of his grace allows him to live. This is true of the community just as it is true of the life of the individual, which through experiences of being tried and being comforted is ever more and more being thrown upon God and committed to his grace.

Our story was from the very first the subject of various typological expositions. A warning must be uttered, however, against a typology which pursues individual material associations instead of holding precisely to the kerygma. Isaac is not simply a type of Christ. (It is true that we also saw christological features in Abraham, who suffered being forsaken by God and who himself surrendered the promise!) Furthermore, it is best not to regard the ram caught in the thicket as a type of Christ.

The author of Hebrews (11:17-19) arbitrarily gives the sacrifice event an interpretation which certainly was far from the mind of the Old Testament author. But this reinterpretation is important, for it identifies the thrust of the New Testament promise which Christians must keep in mind in all their moments of affliction: the resurrection of the dead and the new life which is promised to us in Christ.

Genesis 32:22-33

If in preaching on Old Testament texts the expositor wishes to find a rewarding and new point of departure, he must not shrink from becoming as familiar as possible with the character and nature of his text. The story of Jacob, too, is a highly artistic composition combining very diverse, separate traditions, and this composition is clearly marked by two narratives which by virtue of their programmatic content stand out from all the others and thus provide, in a thematic respect, a decisive and distinctive stamp to the whole: these two are the Bethel story and the Peniel story. In both of them the paradoxical character of the divine action is as sharp as can be imagined. At the point where everything seems to be lost, where the blessing seems to have turned into a curse, the paternal blessing is renewed for the refugee. And at the point where we see Jacob returning home in prosperity, where only his relationship with Esau remains to be set in order, there God attacks him by night, like some nocturnal apparition.

It is well known that as to its materials, the story as a local (cultic?) tradition goes back to the earliest pre-Israelite times. But the preacher needs to keep this in mind only to the extent that there are narrative elements of great antiquity which have been seized and saturated by the faith of Israel. Thus in the exposition of the final version of such a narrative, not all the elements in the story can be adduced and utilized, at least not all of them to an equal extent. "There is yet a remnant that does not come out right" (Baumgärtel). This story likewise does not purport simply to relate the experience of an individual; instead, it exhibits an obvious transparency to what is collective and communal. In fact, it contains the explicit identification "You shall be called Israel." In this story Israel has expressed something of her own history with God; and, further, she has set forth her relationship to God in the picture of that nocturnal struggle with the God who feigns a frightful mien yet promises an ultimate bestowal of blessing. In the primitive vessel of that story Israel actually is letting us see something of her experience with God, an actual experience of her being guided by him. Therein lies the unassailably historical character of the story for the believer.

Jacob is preoccupied with preparations for his encounter with Esau; this is clearly indicated by verse 22 and the whole of the preceding narrative. He still dreads that encounter, and going through it appears to him to be the last great task of his pilgrimage. But he must go through a still more trying encounter: "A man wrestled with him there." The focus of interest of the story is not the earthly appearance of this man—we must think here of an angelic figure—in view of the fact that in and behind him the Lord God is dealing with Jacob in the most direct way. Now this is a struggle that Jacob has to go through entirely alone, one in which no "gift" (vs. 21) will help him to change his adversary's attitude. But Jacob accepts the struggle, and it may be that even in the Israelite version of the story there is still something of awe and admiration at the courage and great strength of their ancestor. Calvin speaks of an "imprudent boldness" (insana temeritas). "Words will not suffice to tell us what the struggle was like. Only those who have tasted such an experience know; no one else will understand it" (Luther). But evidently Jacob only gradually discovers, in the course of the struggle, who it is with whom he is contending. And then there arises in him a strange desire.

For an understanding of Jacob's question in verse 30, we must remember that ancient man was conscious that his life was surrounded and molded by divine powers which he could not decipher. Unless a divine being were to reveal itself to him, he would have no knowledge of the divine world that threateningly encircled him. If he encountered a *numen*, the most elemental question was the question of that being's name, that is, the question of its nature and intentions. Then it could be grasped, one could lay hold upon it; for if one knew the name, one could address this being; one could (by means of an offering) put it under obligation, demand of it a blessing, and indeed perhaps even practice magic with its name (on this point cf. particularly Judg. 13). Our story shows that there is no difficulty great enough to eradicate from human nature this primitive desire to have God at man's disposal. Indeed, this desire is on the increase! Thus in this most urgent of all human questions are interwoven all the plight of man and all his audacity in relation to God. But God eludes his grasp, refusing to give his name, and thus maintains his mystery and his freedom (cf. Exod. 3:13-14). He did not deliver himself into Jacob's hands as the latter had wished. But God also exhibits his freedom in his blessing of Jacob! And therewith the night of testing recedes. *"Num tu is es?"*—thus Luther has Jacob speaking—*"Ei, du himmlischer Vater und Herr. Ego putavi esse spectrum . . . tu ergo es benedictor"* ("Is it you? Ah, you, heavenly Father and Lord. I thought you were a ghost . . . and you are the one who blesses.") "And when he passed Peniel, the sun rose."

But is this blessing supposed to mean that Jacob practically constrained the angel, that he struggled with God and prevailed? Karl Barth (*Church Dogmatics*, I, 2, 338) has sought to understand this as a "great distinction, but at bottom a shattering one." Here is exhibited a man who is always hostile toward grace, who makes a show of strength toward God and is not willing to be strong in his weakness (II Cor. 12:9ff.). We have indicated above how

42

really ambiguous this struggle appears. But the sense of verse 29 now is a positive one: Jacob accepted the battle and held fast to the deity in this its most profound hiddenness. There is in Jacob something of the *anaideia*, the "unabashed pleading," that Jesus pictured as pleasing to God (Luke 11:8). Thus an additional name is given to the patriarch to supplement his earthly name, which in fact contains a bad connotation (25:26; 27:36), "an accusation" (Procksch). This new name recognizes God as the source of his life and existence. Calvin explains Jacob's victory by saying that in our afflictions God naturally does not let his full power be seen.

The event of Jacob's trial has two results: first, Jacob emerges from the struggle as a cripple. Second, linked to what happened that night is a miraculous change in Esau's attitude, though of course we cannot clearly discern the connection that produces the change. The brother who threateningly approaches with a band of four hundred men (32:7) meets Jacob in such a way that the latter believes he sees in Esau "the face of God" (33:10). This expression points to the hidden connection with Peniel.

Thus this story, of which Hosea 12:5 echoes a somewhat different tradition, essentially gives the denouement of the entire Jacob narrative. However, one still can speak only conditionally of a subjective purification and refinement that actually happened to Jacob that he now "is like God intended him to be" (Dillmann). At any rate, it will not do in the exposition of this story to put all the emphasis on this catharsis of the patriarch, for the sake of the honor of Jacob.

In dealing with this text the preacher has a wide-open opportunity to speak to the congregation about the conflicts which beset men because of God's hiddenness and before which modern man stands so helpless. Here it is shown how God can be so profoundly hidden even from those who are called, in fact precisely from them, that they no longer

43

are sure whether they have been delivered into the hands of God or handed over to the malice of an utterly nameless power. The story teaches that such conflicts arise incalculably. They are life-and-death struggles, and in such a night neither skills nor possessions can come to a man's aid. Such contests must be accepted, and they contain a great promise; for in all that is unfathomable God wills to let man cling to him. To be sure, God also will again and again refuse that desire on man's part to capture God and place him at man's disposal; he will not allow infringements upon his freedom and his mystery. Yet he will not thrust man away from himself, and will bless him at the break of day.

Thus the story certainly tells of something much more comprehensive than a "struggle in prayer"; it tells of struggles with the *Deus Absconditus* that largely shape the entire course of man's (and the community's) relationship with God, struggles that naturally then bestow upon prayers their necessity and their promise. And, finally, we may speak of how those who go through such struggles do not emerge from them as "unbroken" as they entered them. It appears that they have paid a price somewhere, in a very vital spot. In various respects Christians are tormented with the thought that in comparison with imposing and impressive persons who are utterly pagan they so often come off quite poorly. Here we are admonished not to be ashamed, but rather to regard this distinctive crippling almost as an honor, as the visible sign of our having been touched by God.

"Thus we have this noble chapter. In it you see the marvelous counsel: this is the way God deals with his saints. It is for our comfort and for an example to us, [showing] that we should constantly keep in mind whether God is also dealing with us in such a way that we should be equipped and ready for such experiences" (Luther).

Genesis 50:20

Literarily considered, the story of Joseph is unmistakably distinguished from the stories of Abraham and Jacob by a much greater unity. Even though all sorts of preliminary stages in this case may also be discerned from its present form, still it must be understood as a sequence of events of much greater internal unity. Here each chapter does not have its own kerygmatic scope; rather, in the theological respect it is striking how rarely and sparingly the narrative speaks of God, and these very few passages—actually only 45:5 ff. and 50:20—then are simply the points of departure and conclusion for the exposition of the larger whole.

Thus the story of Joseph portrays, with an epic breadth that is unusual in the Bible, the nature and the ways of men. All through lengthy chapters we see nothing but what these men are like: how they deal with each other and how they consequently must suffer at each other's hands. In the incidents of fraternal strife and stubborn preference for favorite sons the shadow of the story of Jacob is clearly discernible. Joseph, of course, is "the noblest figure in Genesis" (Procksch). But since even his portrait at the beginning of the story is not entirely irreproachable, in a certain sense one will have to speak of an ensuing purification.

And now the events become entangled in ever new conflicts! It is true that here and there we think we can see a retributive hand at work—in the exaltation of Joseph, in the humbling of his brothers, and so on—but this remains rather an anonymous, impersonal Nemesis in the course of events, one such as Greek antiquity liked to point out. Only at the conclusion (if we except the preparatory words in 45:5), after the death of the old father, does the question of guilt, which once again has arisen (50:15), lead to a

45

solution and disclosure of the secret. Our text is the true interpretative key to the entire Joseph story. It tears away the veil that previously covered all the events and shows how it was God who had been directing everything for good; even where no man could see it, God had kept all the threads in his own hands. But how? A miracle had not occurred, there had been no setting aside of a sphere for a special divine action; instead, the causal chain of human action was completed without a break. But it is to be perceived with amazement and reverence how God has woven his redemptive action into all the grim and savage human action and, indeed, into the evil intentions of the human heart. Evil was not able to frustrate God's plans; rather, it was made to serve the realization of those plans. Both Luther and Calvin strongly emphasize that this does not imply a justification of evil. But neither may we on the other hand analyze the deeds in such a way as to say that God had relaxed the restraints on the wickedness of men in order then to make use of it later (Calvin: "*Neque . . . Deus . . . fraena hominum malitiae laxavit, ut hac occasione postea utereter*").

Such an almost programmatic theological affirmation about God's relation to evil compels the preacher to take a clear position and clearly dissociate himself from false teachings. The opinion that evil in some form must yet mysteriously be made to serve the good and, indeed, that evil itself is productive of good—this relativizing of evil is quite ancient. Of course the preacher will not be so likely to encounter it in the classical form of idealism, which could praise the fall of man as the most fortunate hour in human history because in it man was for the first time given the possibility and the necessary precondition of a decision for the good (Schiller). He is more likely to meet it in the opinion that evil, too, is an inalienable aspect of life, for life becomes rich and full only for one who has also passed

46

through the depths of guilt (cf. Dehmel's poem about the three rings). But still much more prevalent is the thoughtless and godless saying that is heard in connection with calamities: "Who knows what good it may bring?" It is as though there is something like a conformity to law that is inherent in the world, that out of evil good must come, and that there is something like a secret creative power in evil to cause good! Here we are dealing with what is obviously an ancient and now fully secularized element of the Christian faith. Wrongly appropriated by modern man as a "truth," it rightly can only be accepted from God's hand as a miracle.

Salvation came out of great sin only when Christ was nailed to the cross, and our text could be written as the great interpretative key to the story of Christ's passion and resurrection. Thus the story of Joseph is nothing but a signpost, a preparation for the miracle that God has bestowed in Christ. Is there not also a finger pointing to Christ in the strict exclusiveness of the contrast "You . . . God"? For who but Christ could utter this saying in such a unilateral fashion? Yet everyone must also include himself in it. Calvin certainly is correct: this saying also prompts the one who utters it to look into his own heart ("Ut . . . arcanis Dei judiciis admonitus in se ipsum descendat, seque ad officium hortetur"). It is undoubtedly true that the consciousness expressed in 50:20, according to our story, humbles Joseph and constrains him to an attitude of submission. "Am I in the place of God?" (Luther's translation, "I am under God," is likely improper.) This means that after God has spoken and acted decisively in the matter, Joseph may not give room any longer to his (possibly still hostile) feelings. How much more must that hold true for all our conflicts, now that God has spoken and acted decisively in Christ! But God's word still preserves a stringent clarity, and it does not cloak evil in a wrongly

47

understood conciliatory attitude, nor does it bestow a halo upon evil.

Genesis 50:20 is the word of a backward look. It is not uncommon to hear or to read spiritual biographies that, in looking back on the lifespan involved, presume to set forth God's ways and plans even to details. But it must be asked whether that does not go beyond the competence of our faith, whether our life can yet be revealed to us now in its unity as it is planned by God. Our life is still hidden with Christ in God. But when Christ who is our life is revealed, then we shall also be revealed with him (Col. 3:3). We have in fact seen that at the very end of the Joseph story the veil falls away from the unwholesomely interwoven events and ways. So also only at the end will an overview be granted to us, in the bright clarity of the new life. Until then we can only believe, in the strict sense of the saying, that "for those who love God, all things work for their good" (Rom. 8:28).

Joshua 1:1-9

New Year's

Crucial for the understanding of this text is the definition of the place in salvation history of the one who is being addressed here. What lies behind him, and what lies before him?

Since early times Israel has celebrated the memory of God's deeds that have established the redemptive relationship between Israel and God. She has preserved the memory of these deeds partly in poetic hymns (Ps. 136), and partly in prose, in confessionlike summaries. However, the most comprehensive presentation of this course of history—it extends from Abraham down to Israel's entering into Canaan—is the Hexateuch itself (the Old Testament books from Genesis through Joshua). In it Israel has compiled all available documentary and theological material in order to give a portrayal of this unique portion of her history from all angles. The theologies of many periods constructed this massive work, for ultimately it was the obligation of each generation to work out for itself this confession of God's saving acts. In the book of Joshua there are extensive Deuteronomic sections (our text is one of them), that is, deposits of a relatively recent theology. In this very text Israel has given the most mature and most vigorously thought out theological interpretation of the final act of the redemptive history.

In response to our question about the place in salvation history of this discourse we can say: the crucial redemptive acts of God all lie in the past. Israel has been delivered at the Red Sea, has received the commandments, and has been miraculously led in the wilderness. Now there remains only the last step, the emergence into the final fulfillment, the occupation of the Promised Land and entrance into rest (Josh. 1:13, 15; 21:44). Thus God's address to Joshua comes in an actual interim period, between promise and fulfillment, between election and the ultimate condition of salvation. This divine discourse presupposes that Israel—at the very borders of the Promised Land—has reached a critical point, and it shows that a great deal still can happen—for ill as well as for good—even in this last stage of her journey; for all those acts of God in the past do not rule out the possibility that Israel still could come to grief just before the final fulfillment. The undertone of concern that Israel could still forfeit her salvation cannot be ignored in this discourse. The pathos of this address, marked throughout by the air of a departure, lies in the admonition to make this final portion of the journey aright.

The text is essentially in good shape. Luther's Bible has more correctly translated the we^emets in verse 6 as "be undismayed," and in verses 7 and 9 as "be joyous." In verse 4 we should read "as far as Lebanon." As to form, this text is a discourse in which God speaks to Joshua, a conversation with the one who now bears the responsibility for the people of God. But as to contents, the discourse is close to those Levitical war sermons which according to Deuteronomy 20:2 were actually delivered in those times (an example is found in Deut. 9:1-6). Such wars were regarded as sacral events, because God himself was the actual active participant; it was he who fought, and to him alone belonged the spoils. For men participation was rather a matter of confession and of their faith (Judg. 7:2ff.).

How critical was the situation between election and fulfillment is shown especially by the story of the revolt that erupted after the return of the spies (Num. 14). At that time the people first became fully aware of what they had committed themselves to when they submitted themselves to this God, and now they yearned for the apparent security of Egyptian slavery. Our text even concedes that on this last leg of the journey there were the possibilities of being frightened and dismayed (vs. 9), all the more since just at this point Israel can no longer draw comfort from the leadership, the miracles, and the intercession of Moses. But —and this is the main idea of the text—there is no reason to be dismayed, for God has already made provision for everything; every footbreadth of land that their feet will tread on this road to final fulfillment has already been promised to them by God (the "I have given" is the so-called perfect tense of a contract). We must hear from verses 3-5 the inconceivable authorization that they contain. Is there not something in them of I Corinthians 3:21 ("All things are yours")? Every step of the way is smoothed, and every show of resistance is already broken.

50

That Deuteronomist transmitter of the tradition to whom we owe these verses saw reality no less clearly than do we; Israel's cheerless situation among her enemies in the time of the exile, when he was writing, could not be hidden from his view. But that did not hinder him from presenting this progress of God's people toward the ultimate fulfillment in terms of its glory, a glory of divine guidance which can only be believed. (Our faith is less demanding; it is already satisfied if it is allowed to discern the next step as directed by God.) Actually verses 3 and 5 move along in an exalted feeling of confidence that almost takes away our breath. Here, however, what is involved is not the individual way of this or that man, but the way of the entire people of God into their rest; and it may be said of this people that God accompanies them, indeed, that in every respect he has already prepared the way for them; he has considered every footstep.

This assurance is followed (the sequence is not unimportant!) by the admonition to be faithful to the "book of this Torah." Our word "law" is an inaccurate translation of the word "Torah," for the latter refers to something altogether different from a "law book." In this literature the word "Torah" means the sum of all the beneficent divine intention for Israel. In theological terms it includes both gospel and law. Israel is to continue in a constant inner dialogue with the contents of this book; she is never to cease reflecting upon it and speaking of it. Here we are not far from Psalm 119, which speaks in unending variation of how this revelation of God's will is the content of man's spiritual life and how it concerns man's capacity for thought just as much as the will and the feelings. In fact, there is an active faith only where it relates everything that man encounters or experiences to this book of divine revelation. It is not that everything alike is always included or covered in it, but that this book is meant to keep us

51

spiritually alert; we are to stay in dialogue with it and to talk about it.

The conclusion in verse 8 can cause some difficulties for us, because it offers the opinion that the keeping of the commandments is more profitable than disobedience, even in external and practical respects. But Christians also held this belief as late as the dawning of the modern period! In a society that is still ordered by Christian principles, it is inevitable that the law-abiding, the helpful, the peaceable person is held in high regard in civil life also. Today we are persuaded first by the negative side of the matter: practical wisdom tells us that transgressing the commandments is unwise because thereby man injures himself, his family, and his relations with others. The ancients, however, held the view that evil, like good, is a very real power in life and that it is a matter of human wisdom to ban the disruptive powers and to keep the beneficent ones active. Our text is, to be sure, a speech uttered by God; however, it is not addressed to the people at large, only to their leader; it is something like a set of instructions given to one who has a special commission. Accordingly, it pertains more to the fundamental and general theological matters. In the speech which Joshua then made to the people (vss. 10 ff.), a much more practical direction is taken (instructions about provisions for the journey, etc.). The preacher, too, must bear this in mind.

It is possible to preach on such a text as this only when one is able to perceive that the redemptive event that is spoken of here is so closely connected with the Christian redemptive event that the Christian ideas allow expression in the words of the Old Testament. It will not suffice to be able merely to enumerate with respect to what is common to the two Testaments only a few basic ideas about the God-man relationship, for example, sin, atonement, and redemption. What is involved is rather the question of

52

whether God's dealings with Israel and the situation into which Israel came through these dealings are so closely connected with the New Testament Christ event that even the Old Testament words can be heard by us, in our Christian status in life, as instruction. Applied to our text, that would mean that in that situation of setting out for the final fulfillment of the people of God we can recognize and perceive ourselves, although the blessings of salvation toward which the new Israel is moving are not the same.

I Kings 19:1-18
Fifth Sunday After Trinity

To end this pericope with verse 7, as originally proposed, creates some difficulties; for in thus limiting the length of the text neither the real reason for Elijah's despair can become clear enough (in fact, Elijah first expresses it in vs. 10!), nor can the judgment and the comfort that God discloses to the prophet be voiced. If one takes the entire narrative (vss. 1-18) as a text, its contents could exceed the scope of a single sermon; but in view of the fact that one can easily focus the sermon on the main event, this difficulty is not as grave as the task of having to preach solely on the beginning of a story that comes to grips with its real subject only beyond the endpoint of the text.

I

The story must once have existed as an independent unit. Only later was it combined with the Carmel story by means of two introductory verses. Actually both stories (chaps. 18 and 19) treat approximately the same theme, namely Yahweh's self-disclosure in a situation of utter hopelessness. Through this combining of the two, the story in chapter 19 loses some of its psychological motivation, for Elijah's despair is difficult to explain after the preceding miracle on Mt. Carmel.

When Jezebel notifies Elijah of her intention to have him slain within twenty-four hours, she is in effect making a diplomatic proposal that offers both parties a way out: Elijah is given the opportunity to escape her intention by taking flight, and she is potentially relieved of having to follow through with her threat. (One can reflect on whether Elijah in accepting this suggestion was unfaithful to his commission and was thus quite logically bound to fall from the safety of his charisma into a state of fear and insecurity.)

The passage in verses 9-14 has obviously been disarranged by doublets. It becomes more clear if we excise verses 9b-11a from the original components as an awkward anticipation. The theophany itself contains a serious and not yet satisfactorily explained difficulty. How is it to be explained that Yahweh does not appear in the storm, the earthquake, or the fire, but in the still, small voice? The symbolic interpretation preferred earlier, according to which Yahweh is not made manifest in the wild elemental forces but in gentleness and quietness, and according to which therefore Elijah was being instructed about God's gracious purpose (not yet adequately recognized by the prophet), is to be abandoned in any case. Quite apart from the fact that storm, earthquake, and fire, as well as the quiet stirring, are only circumstances accompanying the following commission, this passage says nothing at all about God's gentle and quiet rule in history. In my opinion the contrast lies somewhat on the same plane as the Deuteronomic paraeneses in Deuteronomy 5:26 and 4:11ff., where the earlier Sinai tradition is interpreted to mean that at Sinai Israel's experience was exclusively one of hearing and thus that the actual revelational event is uniquely reduced to the pronounced and audible word. But however considerable may be the theological concerns that the narrator expresses in this undoubtedly unique portrayal of a theophany, still the expositor must not lose sight of the gradation in rank; for the crucial thing in the entire portrayal of the theophany is the speech addressed by God to Elijah.

II

The story depicts assaults upon the spirit (and indeed a case of deep despair) by which Elijah was tormented. [1] It was a crucial turning point when in the first decades of the present century theology learned anew to grasp the concept of these assaults (*Anfechtungen*), particularly in Luther's testimonies about his own experience. These assaults are something entirely different from "occupational hazards" of the life of faith. They are, rather, integrating forces in our Christian existence. Man needs them, for without them there is no true knowledge of Christ. "Afflictions of this kind are highly beneficial to us. They are not destructive, as indeed they seem to be; they are instructive; and every Christian will realize that without afflictions he could not learn to know Christ [that is, Christ's significance]. . . .

[1] Even at such a depth of despair, in Israel people knew their lives to be so encompassed by Yahweh that the possibility of removing one from among the living lay in the hands of Yahweh alone. The meaning of Elijah's reference to his fathers ("I am no better than my fathers") is not really clear. It is possible that by this he means to say that even in the time of the fathers, when belief in God had not yet been eroded, he would not have been equal to such a situation.

55

Thus afflictions guard one against pride, and at the same time they advance one's knowledge of Christ" (Luther, TR I, 141; cf. *WA* 40/1, 50, 1). Thus Luther could even say that the greatest affliction would be to have no afflictions. Perhaps in our sorrows and our despair we are closer to Christ than we know; perhaps in them we are more pleasing to God than in our "cheerful courage of faith" and our so often dubious "nevertheless" of faith! In this area the theology of the community has been deficient in providing consolation. Luther made a clear distinction among the various kinds of trials: there are those caused by sin, by the law, by fear, by predestination, by the sacrament, and not least of all by the *tentatio mortis* (on this point one may recall the medieval dance of death). The perceptive shepherd of souls today probably would arrive at some different formulations.

Of course for Luther the severest trials were those that came directly from God, that is, when God seemed to withdraw his own word of comfort. According to Luther, only the *"summi e sanctis"* are plunged into such trials; in this connection he thought particularly of Genesis 22. And was not Elijah led into such a trial? After all, God himself called him to fight against the heathen infiltration that was issuing from the royal household, and to lead Israel, who had become corrupt and degenerate in belief, back to her God. Now God had left Elijah in the lurch ("They have torn down thine altars and slain thy prophets with the sword, and I alone am left"). Elijah was not weary of life, but, what is even worse, was "weary of God." What comfort is left for a prophet when he has lost God's own comfort and consolation! We nonprophets still can find all sorts of other consolation. Many people have surrounded themselves with such a breadth of assurances and safeguards that they seem hardly to need God's comfort any longer. But for a prophet whose task it was to track down men in their false security and to bring them out of it,[2] there were only the alternatives of the sustaining hand of God or inconceivable terror when he slipped from this hand. The Bible has much to say about such eruptions of terror in the lives of faltering prophets (Jeremiah, in Jer. 20; Moses, in Num. 1).

In his response to God's question Elijah points to his own zeal. What does he mean by this? This much, at least: "I have done my utmost, I have wasted away, and it has been to no avail." Talk about zeal is a biblical theme, and perhaps it is gradually disappearing from our language. It gives us conflicting impressions—attracts as well as repels—but who among us would dare to criticize Elijah? Is he not a unique accusation against us? Of course anyone who strives primarily to bring into balance, in the form of a noble humanism, the nature of man that is pushed and pulled hither and yon by all sorts of forces will view with deep distrust any attempt on man's part to make himself a vessel of divine zeal. Is there not something disruptive about all zeal? Actually the biblical zealots lived constantly in the presence of catastrophes (Moses, Jeremiah, Jehu [II Kings 10:16], the Maccabeans). One of the characteristic features of the zealot, also, is a certain resoluteness that refuses to quail before things that have terrified whole generations. To the impartial view zealots appear for the most part as destroyers. No one becomes a zealot by his own decision. The person for whom God prescribes a zealot's life forfeits any life of his own. Humanly speaking he bears a fearful burden, and it is easy to charge the zealot

[2]It is worth reflecting upon that there is also a false "securitas" with reference to the Bible. Julius Schniewind once pointed out that "through historical study and research, everything that appeared 'certain' has become uncertain. And for that very reason we now are confronted by the gospels and the apostolic writings precisely as were the first hearers themselves. These likewise had no guarantees of any sort that the message, the gospel, was true" (Zur Erneuerung des Christenstandes [Göttingen: Kleine Vandenhoeck-Reihe 226/227, 1964], p. 42).

with human derelictions and indeed with inhuman behavior. In Psalm 69:8 ff. something like a portrait of the
zealot is sketched: he has become a stranger to his own
brothers, an alien to his mother's sons. Reproaches directed
against God fall back upon him; his soul is tormented; he
suffers inward strife; and he becomes the object of the
scoffers' ridicule. But perhaps God must from time to time
set up among men such signs, and it may be that they, like
Elijah, in their very misfortunes bear a witness for God that
cannot be forgotten.

III

God's response passes over Elijah's assertion that in his
zeal he has done his utmost. It really is not very surprising
that even in our most astute prognoses about the future of
the people of God on earth we always miss the mark. It is
very surprising, however, that this happened also to Elijah,
who knew more than others about God and his people. The
lament that he pours out before God at Horeb can be
summed up thus: "I am the last one who knows the true
God, and it makes no sense any more to fight against the
ascendant paganism." The divine response appears at first
to agree with this. Actually the orders that introduce
Elijah's relief from his office open up a vista of sternest
judgment. God himself will seize and sift his people. From
God himself will issue strokes against his people that could
be regarded as annihilating (Dan. 11:32-36) and having an
impact even on world politics. (We may reflect on what it
may have meant for an Israelite to anoint as king the
Aramean king in Damascus, the mortal enemy of Israel!)
Here it becomes clear what Luther meant when he
occasionally said that God will execute his work "in

disguise" and "behind a mask." Elijah himself now will have to set in motion these annihilating impulses, for judgment begins at the house of God (I Peter 4:17).

Nevertheless this commission from God puts the prophet in the wrong, for God already sees seven thousand who have not bowed the knee—it is idle to ask whether this means a large number or a small one!—as the foundation for a new people of God.

Here we can apply to Elijah what P. Krusche (*Deutscher Evangelischer Kirchentag* [Köln: Kreuz-Verlag, 1965], pp. 110-11) says in his exposition of the prophet Jonah:

> We overestimate the role that we play in the changing situations of history into which God leads us. Here, where it would really matter, we suddenly are lacking a healthy detachment from ourselves! What we need is a little modesty, a little smile, when it is a matter of our theology or of the preservation of our faith in the everyday affairs of life. . . . Could it be that we are not the central figures on whom everything depends? Is it possible that we do not always bear the whole burden of responsibility on our frail shoulders? God—so we have heard—is not interested solely in Jonah, nor even solely in the church, but his concern reaches much farther. . . . And perhaps our anxiety will diminish if we more positively and more thankfully acknowledge what God is doing beyond the walls of the church.

A sermon on this text can only address people who are beset by afflictions and anxieties in view of the existence of the church in our present time and the rapidly changing situation. The sermon must not minimize the dead seriousness of the prospect of judgment (has not our preaching become unworthy of belief primarily because it has been able to speak only of God's "quiet, gentle whispering"?). Nevertheless, the sermon must counter any and all melancholy with the assurance that any human calculation about the future of God's people on earth is idle speculation. Is not the world occupied with monitoring the church's pulse and setting forth a prognosis about its continued existence? Even the most astute of these observations are far from having any connection with God's thoughts and plans. This consolation would have to have a place in the sermon's conclusion (no one will wish to infer from this that the church nevertheless does not demand our keenest vigilance and utmost commitment!).

II Kings 5:1-19
Second Sunday After Trinity

This story—it belongs to the category of legends about the prophets—is set into the context of the Elisha narratives without any specific topical connection. It is not located in chronological terms. At the center of the story stands Elisha, or rather his dealings with a Gentile. But Elisha is not relativized as a member of a particular group or a particular line of succession; he is, rather, at least for his time, *the* all-sufficient helper (vs. 3). Nevertheless the story leads (as moving from the circumference to the center) at first only slowly to him and to the healing that he effects. The sermon also, in its outline, will be guided by this way that has been marked out in advance.

Verses 1-2 form the exposition: Naaman is a highly placed and just man and thus one of those "noble pagans" who so readily become stumbling blocks to the church. Actually the statement that God gave "victory" to the Syrians through him (the Syrians were a kind of ancestral enemy of Israel) involves a major concession. It implies that

God looks upon these just persons, causes them to achieve something, and a beneficent, orderly effect issues from them. Because of them God blesses entire nations. The special thing that God makes happen to Naaman goes far beyond this, for Naaman is a leper. It was not merely an instance of ultimate fulfillment or a splendid consummation. Naaman was stricken with something dreadful; he was a sure prey to death.

The first instrument God employed for this man's deliverance is a "little girl." (There is a temptation to say a word here about the significance of the so-called little people in the household of the church.) But the stimulus that is provided leads to an action on the governmental level, an action that demonstrates a total lack of understanding. In Aram people do not know that gifts of divine grace are bestowed outside the hierarchy of the human order of society; and in response to the question "Am I God?" it must be said that those who do not know the living God still share that same conviction. God had chosen a way to make himself known through an obscure person, while men choose a way exactly opposite to this, by way of the highest officials; and the matter proceeds hopelessly along this latter road. Once again God must intervene and guide matters. But when the great, wretched Naaman with his entire entourage appears at the door of Elisha's hut, he is not even granted a personal reception.

The collision of the two worlds was an uncompromising one. Naaman had anticipated a ceremonial scene with all sorts of mystical hocus-pocus and had hit upon the idea (which has also become current again in modern times!) that there are myths and numinous powers in Damascus as well; indeed, as far as the magic of dark mysteries and of mythical unveilings is concerned, Damascus is superior to Israel. Let the church take heed that she does not attempt to enter into competition with paganism in this area!

This is precisely what Elisha intended to show Naaman, that these mystical cravings are not the road by which man comes to God and to his salvation. Elisha intended to offer a fundamental disappointment to this hankering for magic. Nowhere in the Bible does the water of the Jordan have a sacral quality; it is water "like the cattle drink." The intention is not that one myth should be replaced or surpassed by another; the main concern here is the issue of obedience. In all the yearning for magical miracles Naaman still basically wanted to *understand* it all and to remain above it with his head, in order to keep the matter under his own control! Now he is supposed to humble himself and submit, and never before had he encountered such a demand. It is an act of penitence that Elisha demands of Naaman. Once again simple people enter the picture. The process of healing is described matter-of-factly, and with less interest in the marvelous character of the event than in its completeness.

In light of the absoluteness and strictness of devotion that Naaman observes in Elisha, his gratitude is overshadowed by the concern over whether he would be able to remain in the service of the Lord, and he expresses a twofold wish for a dispensation.

1. The request for a load of "sacred" soil has been a disappointment to many expositors. Was he in fact so little cured of his old notions? This is not a very promising beginning, is it? Yes, it is! The motivation of this request is the concern whether in the outside world his infant faith will simply be smothered by the overwhelming paganism. Hence—obviously in the awareness of his weakness—he seeks to borrow something of the sacred; he seeks for his faith a certain security, for he wants this soil in a certain sense as an insulation against the inroads of paganism (or of profaneness?). Of course it is very important for the church to see this request in its contemporary relevance.

We, too, borrow from the sacred: the style of our church buildings, our "spiritual" songs, the liturgical language, the gestures of the preachers—all this and much else we use (in freedom!) as a similarly insulating layer against the oppressive and insistent outside world. Even without all this we would still have to manage, and we do manage; but where we can have them they are a support and stay for our faith.

2. Much more doubtful is the second request: Naaman's high position as an official will not allow him to detach himself totally from paganism. On certain occasions the ceremony of the court demanded that he take part in the cult of the god Rimmon.

Elisha's answer, intently awaited, is the absolute climax of the story. The preacher must pause here and dwell on this, yet must take care that its unique and striking brevity and reserve—and love—are not talked to death ("And he looked at him and loved him"). The answer is not yes or no; but neither is it an evasion. Its main feature is that it does not establish any kind of law for Naaman. How sharply the prophet had humbled this man, conceding nothing to him; and now he dismisses him with utter generosity, utterly without any rules and regulations—with a benediction! ("I have not found such faith in Israel"). He sends him forth into all the destitution of paganism and leaves him with his faith.

Thus the story of Naaman is neither a cheap miracle story nor a cheap conversion story. Things are by no means all in the clear for Naaman. Problems are indicated that lie beyond what is told. But Naaman's beginning was a promising one.

The sermon can hardly close without a brief mention of the conclusion (vss. 19b-27) as a dark parallel in contrast. Gehazi is not a scoundrel, but he cannot resist the temptation; he, too, desires just once to be great and rich in the world's sight (vs. 23b), and he knows well enough that his master will not countenance that. The ambitious man presents as absurd a picture as the church when it lets itself be tempted to lead a similar double life, knowing all the while that her Lord would never countenance such.

The sermon will first simply relate this biblical story, which probably is largely unknown to the congregation. This establishes the structure of the sermon. On this text there is hardly any need for weighty theological explanations of the relationship of what is provisional in the Old Testament to what is final in the New Testament. The entire salvation story in a typological respect is so obvious (the deliverer, the futile human effort at establishing a connection, the rejection of the desire for magic as the demand for a sign, deliverance, and the first glimpses into the new life) that only at the end is there any need for a further word that will lift the Old Testament witness above its purely immanental character. With respect to a typological exposition of the washing commanded for Naaman as a reference to baptism, suggested by Luther's translation of verse 14, cautious reserve is recommended.

II Chronicles 20

Cantate

Behind this story there lies, in the history of tradition, a cluster of very distinctively formed and sharply delineated conceptions of belief. The story pictures a "holy war." The holy war was an institution of the highest cultic rank. It was begun with sacrifices and inquiries addressed to God (I Sam. 28:6; 30:7; II Sam. 5:19, 23). Those who participated in the undertaking were, because in a peculiar sense standing in the sphere of influence of an utterly nonmediated divine event, subject to specific ritual commandments (I Sam. 21:6; II Sam. 11:11). The one actually active in the holy war was God alone (Josh. 10:14; Judg. 4:14), and therefore the size of the army did not matter; more important than armament and military skill was that the participants have an attitude pleasing to God and that they collaborate in faith, in the undertaking (I Sam. 14:6; Judg. 7:3ff.; II Sam. 24:1ff.). The glory of the victory belonged to God alone. The story of Gideon, for example (Judg. 7), is interested in this emphasis in such a way that no room is left for any sort of synergism on the part of the warriors themselves; in the very presence of the enemy they halt and only provide accompaniment (with those most highly unusual gestures) to the divine event that is beginning (Judg. 7:13-14). That is the climactic point in the holy war: a "terror of God" comes over the enemy, a kind of numinous panic, in which the warriors act in utter confusion and destroy each other (Deut. 7:23; Josh. 2:9; 10:10; Judg. 4:15; I Sam. 7:10; 14:15, 20). Thus at the climax of the event the action is unexpectedly taken out of the hands of the believers, and a miracle from God comes down as into a hollow space that is kept scrupulously clean and free from any human activity. After the end of the period of the judges, with the rise of the professional soldiery, the holy war as a cultic institution began to die out; but the constituent ideas and demands of its faith survived, primarily in the preaching of the prophets. Our narrative here is intended essentially to be an admonition to an age that believed itself to have outgrown these old patriarchal ideas. As to form, it is the later narrative style that reflects its background. As to its content, many of the archaic

65

elements have obviously been spiritualized and theologized (cf. the spiritualization of the ancient war cry into a song of praise!).

In the threat posed by the Moabites, Ammonites, and Meunites (cf. the Septuagint and I Chron. 4:41) what is at stake is the very existence of the community (not merely an infringement upon some individual "rights"). (It appears almost as an unintentional bit of humor that in the excitement of the first report an early copyist makes the extent of the threat even greater than it already was. There was nothing in the ancient account about any participation of the "Syrians" (vs. 2); it must instead be read as *'aram 'edom*.) The situation was extremely grave, and it is worthy of note that the king senses it and expresses it as such with great solemnity (vs. 12). But this very helplessness, which then sees itself as utterly dependent upon God's protection, contains great promise. But the king is exemplary most of all in what he does *not* do: he does not hasten to the arms depot to arrange for equipment, and he does not send out envoys to forge treaties of mutual assistance. Instead, he calls the community to repentance, and he prays; and in this prayer he submits himself entirely to God's protection. (The very people past whom God earlier led the community in his strange plan for history now emerge as the enemy. It is important that the community in its prayer should be able to testify that it has a clear conscience in relation to its enemies!)

But praying is not the whole story; the king also gives some very specific orders. Whatever can be done from the side of the community is to be done. The battle is to be accepted and undertaken by all. But the sequence in which things are done is utterly crucial; and where one prays thus, one does not, in the final analysis, expect deliverance to come from human agencies, no matter how conscientiously they are to be utilized.

The prayer is followed immediately by Jahaziel's prophetic declaration: God hears such prayers; and such a community will not lack those who in the hour of peril prophetically give her instruction: "Not by might, nor by power, but by my Spirit" (Zech. 4:6). The first aid that God sends to his community is the assurance that he and not they will wage the battle; and hence they already know which side will be victorious. Here for the first time—very prematurely, in any human evaluation of the situation!—the community voices its song of praise (vss. 18-19).

The same prophet who had announced to the community God's final decision about his readiness to deliver aid now also gives some very practical instructions about where and how to engage the enemy in battle (vs. 16). We have already observed that the community by no means sinks into a state of quietism after having prayed; on the contrary, the people are involved, down to the very last member of the community, in relation to God and in relation to the enemy. In what follows, then, there is a very strange intermingling of the activities—the army's marching forth and the exhortation to absolute faith (in vs. 20b a quotation from Isa. 7:9b), the formation for battle and songs of praise!

Now what actually happens? From a military perspective, it is impossible for the singers to have marched out in front of the armed men (vs. 21), but this shows which activity has priority: it is the second song of praise of the community, in the face of the superior forces of the enemy. The beginning of the song of praise is very closely dovetailed with the intervention of divine aid (vs. 22). The text does not speak of any causal connection. Thus the assistance remains God's free act; but is it not the intention here to show us that praise is the community's real protection (Ps. 9:3)? The narrative certainly understands the $m^e ar^e bim$ (the "ambushers") to be heavenly powers sent by God to intervene and cause the enemy's defeat. In

the confusion that arises the enemy forces attack each
other, the community contributing not so much as a single
stroke of a sword to the victory. They gain a large amount of
booty, and four days later the people gather in the Valley of
Blessing (Berakah) for a third song of praise.

For the Christian community, in Jehoshaphat's place
there stands the one who is king in a fuller sense. After his
resurrection he assumed the rule of which Jehoshaphat
speaks in verse 6. His prayer stands for ours. It is he alone
who actually surveys the situation for us; in him and with
him the community may become poor and may despair of
her strength and her tactics. But he goes with her even into
battle, and he speaks assurance to her; and thus she may
experience the miracle that "joy in the Lord is her strength"
(Neh. 8:10).

The narrative is essentially indivisible. One could let the
reading of the larger text begin with verse 13 and then set
forth the context in the sermon, or, perhaps, read only
verses 1-6, 12, 14-15, and 19-26.

Job 2:1-10

Here is a scene from the prose history of Job. As is well
known, the narrator brings widely diverse settings before
our eyes, as in a drama; and these settings, the earthly scene
and that of the heavenly throne room, alternate. Of course
being on earth Job knows nothing of what has gone before,
that is, the heavenly background of his sufferings. Who is
Job? Curiously, he lives on the outermost periphery of the
people of God; the land of Uz lies in the eastern part of the
region east of the Jordan, and his time cannot be finally

determined from the story. One cannot say that the figure emerges very concretely or with very clear individual features in the poem. It has something about it that is impalpably typical; the whole composition in fact is not an actual history but rather a narrative related for purposes of instruction, which accordingly falls into a certain schematic pattern. Job was an exemplary pious and wealthy man. But the unity of upright behavior and prosperity (regarded by men as so normal!) suffers a puzzling breach. How did this happen?

On one of the audience days in heaven there was a conversation between God and the accuser. "Satan" is a concept of an office and not a proper name (the article indicates this); consequently one should not speak of "the" Satan. He is one of the heavenly beings, of course entrusted by God with a particular function. His task—something like that of the public prosecutor—is to ferret out hidden injustice in the far-flung empire of the heavenly king. And if a person throughout life is regarded as devout and yet basically is not, this matter, too, belongs to the sphere of Satan's office. Now to be sure he does not, in response to God's question, doubt Job's piety in itself, but he poses a question about the man's motives: "Does Job fear God for nought?" (1:9). This question poses the problem of the narrative context, namely whether there is a piety "without reward even in the direst need." God concedes that this is a fair question; evidently its purpose and the accuser's is to keep secure one of God's interests. Thus the sermon should strenuously avoid any suggestion of the dualism of God and the devil. It is also to be noted that the initiative in the conversation lay with God, and that the accuser suggested, "Stretch forth your hand," and at the last Job did not say, "Satan has taken away." Hence the sermon should not be burdened with a problem that the text does not pose or propose to answer. (The dualism of God and accuser is

69

almost rather a technical necessity for narrative purposes; it serves to divide and allocate the different functions in the story.) Hence also the charge in 2:3b is not of crucial importance for the understanding of the whole; it only advances the treatment of the theme: in this one case the skepticism of the accuser was unfounded.

But it is a different matter with the objection offered by the accuser in verse 4. The meaning of the terse phrase—it sounds like a proverb—cannot be framed with utter clarity. It is something like "tit for tat " or, "For man everything is a matter of business" (Hölscher) or, again, "When it comes to a man's own skin, then he will go to any extreme and will abandon all restraints." In any case, both expressions made by the accuser (1:9; 2:4) bear witness to a profound and utterly illusionless knowledge of human nature: in the ultimate crisis a man will throw all ballast overboard. And God allows room for this question too. Thus it came about that Job's sufferings were intensified to an almost unbearable level. This time Job's reaction was different from that in the first round of testing. He does not make a confession (1:21), but (here the narrator is counting on attentive readers) he does something else: silently and without remonstration he withdraws from human society to the refuse heap outside the settlement and resignedly assumes the lot of the leper. It would be possible to think that the story could almost conclude here with this climax in verse 8. But Job's afflictions are intensified still more. He is paid a visit while there outside the settlement. What will his wife say in the presence of this man on the garbage dump? The import of what she says has been obscured only because the commentaries inquire with too much subtlety into the woman's psychological motives, and these are of no interest to the narrator. (For example, it is impermissible to read: Curse "so that . . . ," signifying an attitude prompted entirely by sympathy.) It even appears that the ancient exegetes—Calvin speaks of *"infernalem furiam"*—went too far in their zeal. Is she not rather typical of ordinary pious people, as the accuser knows them, who in their greatest sanctity flare up as injured parties when the withholding of a blessing hinders them in the naïve expansion of their human nature? Job sharply rejects this suggestion. (The word "foolish," or "nonsensical," means more in the Old Testament than it does in our language; there it denotes a defect with respect to morality or faith and is equivalent to "shameful, base." In verse 10 the *'t* following the Hebrew *gam* appears by mistake; it should read *gam 'att,* in order then to begin the next sentence with *'et hattob.)* The sentence "Shall we . . . ," however, is not uttered with great religious feeling; rather it contains an utterly sober reflection, indeed almost a primitive logic of belief: we have on such and such occasions affirmed God as giver and have thanked him. But now nothing has changed in this our confession of God as the Lord of our lives! But it is important above all not to take this sentence (or that of 1:21) as a lofty achievement of self-control; 1:20 has shown that Job is entirely human, vulnerable and desolate; and the voicing of his pain is kept within the bounds of the ordinary. It is incorrect to see in him "a worthy picture of composure and calm" (Duhm). We must not understand him as a man who can grit his teeth and endure hardship better than others can; instead, the most remarkable thing about him is the certainty, indeed even the easy matter-of-factness of his confession. The rhetorical question in 2:10 shows that there is no heroic expenditure of energy behind this confession; no, Job is secure in his belief, utterly free of any problem with it. In that belief—thus the narrator comments much as an epilogist does after the close of an act in a drama—Job did not sin "with his lips."

If the Job story is a didactic narrative, then the lesson it is meant to teach would have to be capable of concise formulation; but that is not at all easy. To conclude that the sufferings of the devout are tests would be to abridge the contents altogether too severely, for the serious question posed in 1:9 then would not receive its due. But if we formulate it thus: "Is there such a thing as selfless piety?"—that too would be inadequate. "With his lips" was the conclusion of our text (vs. 10*b*). Evidently what men *say* in the presence of others about their suffering is of ultimate and crucial significance in God's sight (almost more important than the question of the inward attitude of their souls!). Herder makes a good point with reference to our story: "Things are done above (in heaven), talked about here below." The climactic points in the prose story of Job are the words which the people find to utter; in the context of our passage that means the words of both the wife and the husband, both of them highly significant as types. And here by all means the sermon should pause. Neither of these two persons knows anything of the heavenly prologue that belongs to this provocative story (Its background is neither the impersonal nature of powers or laws nor their arbitrariness!) Ah, how perilous are the words of the people closest to us! It is almost precisely as the accuser had predicted! But now in Job's case it is to be remembered that God had vouched for him in advance; all the angels, who have been in on the conversation with the accuser, now look at Job in suspense: will he confirm God's judgment? Job suffers "to keep the Creator's word of honor about him" (Herder); thus he is a martyr in the New Testament sense, i.e., not because of his suffering but because of the witness he bears.

Hence the Old Testament answers the difficult question in 1:9 thus: "Yes, there is this man." But now this question is curiously theoretical and somewhat vague (didactic narrative!). Who then is this Job? Is he actually the type of a piety that is common in Israel? We noted earlier that he is an "outpost" (Kierkegaard), and that the narrator is not able to identify the time in which he lived at all. While we earlier said that the figure of Job has been given a strongly typical touch by the narrator, now we must speak further of a typological significance that borders on the marvelous: the man who is cast down from great wealth into poverty, the man who as an unclean person leaves the society of other people, the one in whom the all-seeing eye of the accuser finds nothing amiss, the servant of God (vs. 3), the one who has suffered "without cause" (vs. 3b), the one who safely and securely rests in faith is shown in the dialogues, on the other hand, to be a man who is flooded with despair at being forsaken by God! Thus this Job narrative will also have typical significance for those who are baptized into Christ's death. And the "yet spare his life" (vs. 6b) is also spoken by God about their sufferings, in a sense much more comprehensive than is intended here in the Old Testament.

When one generation has served its time, fulfilled its duty, fought its battle, then Job has guided it; when the new generation, with its innumerable ranks and every individual among them in his place, stands ready to begin the journey, then Job is again present, takes his place, which is the outpost of humanity. If the generation sees only happy days and prosperous times, then Job faithfully goes with them, and if, nevertheless, an individual in his thought experiences the terrible, is apprehensive because of his conception of what life may conceal of horror and distress, of the fact that no one knows when the hour of despair may strike for him, then his troubled thought resorts to Job, dwells upon him, is reassured by him. For Job keeps faithfully by his side and comforts him, not as if he had thus suffered once for all what he would never again have to endure, but he comforts him as one who witnesses that the terror is endured, the horror experienced, the battle of despair waged, to the honor of God, to his own salvation, to the profit and happiness of others. In joyful days, in fortunate times, Job walks by the side of the race and guarantees its happiness, combats the apprehensive dream

that some horror may suddenly befall a man and have power
to destroy his soul as its certain prey.

Only the thoughtless man could wish that Job should not
accompany him, that his venerable name should not remind
him of what he seeks to forget, that terror and anxiety exist in
life. Only the selfish man could wish that Job had not existed,
so that the idea of his suffering might not disturb with its
austere earnestness his own unsubstantial joy, and frighten
him out of his intoxicated security in obduracy and perdition.
In stormy times, when the foundation of existence is shaken,
when the moment trembles in fearful expectation of what
may happen, when every explanation is silent at the sight of
the wild uproar, when a man's heart groans in despair, and
"in bitterness of soul" he cries to heaven, then Job still walks
at the side of the race and guarantees that there is a victory,
guarantees that even if the individual loses in the strife, there
is still a God, who, as with every human temptation, even if a
man fails to endure it, will still make its outcome such that we
may be able to bear it; yea, more glorious than any human
expectation. (Soren Kierkegaard, "The Lord Gave, and the
Lord Hath Taken Away," *Edifying Discourses*, trans. David F.
Swenson and Lillian Marvin Swenson [Minneapolis: Augs-
burg Publishing House, 1944], II, 8–9)

Psalm 32

Nineteenth Sunday After Trinity

This psalm belongs to the category of "thanksgiving
psalms" and very clearly exhibits the characteristic features
of that category: (1) a portrayal of the distress, (2) an appeal
to God and experience of deliverance, and (3) thanksgiving
and testimony about the deliverance in the presence of the

congregation. These thanksgiving hymns are all more or less to be understood as fulfillment of a vow that was made in a time of great need, and thus they have a strong confessional character. We have to think of them as presented in the temple, usually in connection with a thank offering. Why should not the sermon render the psalm easy for the congregation to remember by stressing the contours that make it typical of this category? Since it is an indivisible whole, we cannot neglect verses 8 ff. It is not a penitential psalm. Protestant worship has not been able to continue the special cultic tradition that elevated it in the Middle Ages to a place of special significance as one of the seven penitential psalms.

The text is corrupt, and in some places one has the suspicion that the original utterances have been severely altered. The term *maskil* in the superscription is un-explained, but in any case it does not mean "instruction."

If in keeping with our present-day insight the psalm probably is to be understood as a ritual formula (or at least as a free poetic composition) which still strictly adheres to the course of the cultically prescribed schema, then we shall have to abandon the heretofore favored biographical interpretation that relates the psalm to David and his sin (II Sam. 12; according to this view Ps. 32 would follow Ps. 51 in David's experience). Yet with all the restrictions that belong to the type, the psalm is not lacking in par-ticularities; the plight from which the person praying is aware of having been saved is the plight of sin. Further, the diction of the psalm resembles that of wisdom literature; i.e., it is highly didactic. The psalmist strives to sum up his experience in concise, epigrammatic sentences and to expand it into what is universally true. Thus at the beginning and the end there stand, columnlike, sentences saturated with experience (vss. 1-2, 10) which express

75

(ritually?) the essence of the experience of faith not only of an individual but of the whole community. Between these pillars the psalm is divided, broadly speaking, into two parts: first, the confession to God (vss. 3-7), and second, the confession in the presence of others (vss. 8-9).

On the first of these two parts: One does not arrive at this confession by an easy route; the road thence led by way of the ultimately intolerable "silence." The exposition will do well not to attribute this, one-sidedly, to the voice of a bad conscience that would not be stilled. Whether the person voicing the prayer was constantly aware of the true reason for his inward suffering is not very important. What is involved here is a twofold silence—in his own presence and before God. (He calls it "silence" from the perspective of his later enlightenment, as indeed in retrospect from that later position not only a portrayal but an interpretation is given.) At any rate, all peace had fled from him; a "spirit of melancholy" (Luther) encompassed him. The text certainly gives the preacher every opportunity to say something important about the soul's desolations and convulsions created by unconfessed guilt. In this connection we should think not only of the convulsions of the soul as they might concern the psychoanalyst, but also of the philosophical and ideological attempts of man to justify himself. All in all one needs to guard against a one-sided psychologizing, for from this unconfessed sin the psalm derives (indeed especially and in strong terms) grave disturbances of the physical deportment of man. In this way the psalmist is expressing what perhaps is most profoundly declared in Genesis 3, namely that all disruptions and dissonances of our life situation can be traced back to the disruption of our relationship with God. It is not "demons" but God's "hand" that is so heavy upon the suppliant. Thus the guilt, unforgiven because unconfessed, may properly be discussed in terms of its effect upon the actual condition of one's life. And since the psalm bears a strong cultic imprint, a word may also be said about the fact that the community as a whole likewise can see itself confronted with the necessity of a confession of guilt and that healthful effects upon its inward condition may be expected from such confession. Forgiveness, then, coincides with confession. Yet, if the text in this passage is reliable, the suppliant appears to intend to suggest that God does not offer himself to man everywhere and always in the same way: on verse 6b ("at a time of finding") compare Psalm 69:13; Isaiah 55:6; and II Corinthians 6:2. In verse 6 it is declared that forgiveness guarantees complete protection against every threat from the powers of chaos. The Christian can understand this only eschatologically: in this life he is granted a wholly new relationship to suffering and in life to come, redemption and glorification of the body. "Where there is forgiveness of sins, there is also life and blessedness."

On the second part: Beginning with verse 8, the suppliant turns abruptly to his fellowman. (The community obviously is present and is hearing the confession.) Now he is empowered to instruct others. This turning is very significant: what he has experienced from God is not his private affair but concerns the community. Everything hinges on his now not being "dumb" (Ps. 30:12; 22:26). Here we are to learn about the nature of true confession: it corresponds to a divine action that affects us personally and calls us to a decision. Anyone who has experienced such deliverance bears a responsibility before God for others. He must "turn his eyes to them." The character of those who do not heed God's gracious offer is sharply and unsparingly pictured. From the perspective of the enlightenment that has come to the one uttering this prayer they are obstinate and irrational beasts. This was a favorite psalm of Augustine's.

Psalm 96

First Sunday After Epiphany

This psalm belongs (along with 47, 93, 97, 99, and 149, for example) to the group of the so-called enthronement psalms. It is characteristic of them to contain, in an emphatic position, the phrase *Yahweh malak*, "Yahweh has become king" (96:10). They stem from a great cultic festival in which Yahweh's enthronement was celebrated (like the enthronement of earthly kings), and perhaps it was even represented in a cultic mime. In any case the enthronement was made visibly manifest in a procession (Ps. 24), in the entrance into the temple. If the rejoicing even at the enthronement of earthly kings was such "that the earth was split by the noise" (I Kings 1:40), at this festival it certainly was not otherwise; and indeed all these psalms are marked by the loftiest rejoicing. The kingdom which Yahweh assumes is the world, which thereby is brought again under the greatness, the power, and the blessing of its creator. Thus in these psalms there are dominant—something surprising in the chorus of Old Testament witnesses!—the elements of the first article of faith. It is biblically and theologically significant that the concept of the gospel (in Old Testament language *besora*) has its ultimate cultic origin here. Actually *bissar* means to deliver the message that Yahweh has entered upon his rule; the *mebasser* was perhaps a kind of cultic herald who at the climactic point of the festival announced the consummation of the enthronement (Isa. 52:7). Hence the imperative *basseru* in verse 2b must not be overlooked by the expositor (Septuagint: *Euangelizesthe!*).

At first only the elect community knows of this cosmic turning point that has come about; this knowledge is both its blessing and its commission (Isa. 40:9-10; 60:1 ff.). Thus it has a twofold obligation: (1) that of praise, and (2) that of proclamation to the world. (In essence the two cannot be separated.)

On the first of these two: The community is to sing the "new song." The new song (cf. Pss. 33:3; 98:1; 149:1; Isa. 42:10) is just the song that hymns God's enthronement. And in fact among the innumerable songs that men have sung and will sing, there is only one that really is new and timely, namely the one that declares that God has entered upon his kingly rule. All others stand under the verdict of Ecclesiastes 1 ("What is it that has happened? Precisely what will happen again hereafter, and there is nothing new under the sun" [Eccl. 1:9]). But this message is not only new, it is also inexhaustible; and it is framed ever anew. Every day it must be spoken forth (vs. 2b).

At first glance it will be surprising that the psalm has nothing at all to say about what is unsolved, i.e., about the suffering and the enigmas of this world. But this disregard for what is so obvious to the natural man is not a matter of conquering self or of exercising pious discipline, but rather an expression of security. If God has assumed his rule, if one now knows definitively who is supreme in this world, then everything is already decided; everything is good, and then there is no grumbling of any sort. All true praise lives out of the certainty of the eschatological kingdom; it does not stop at what is subjected to our human calculation, but it knows that already even now the kingdom belongs to God. It knows that someday we shall utter praise even about that which now distresses us. Therein, then, the earthly community is also united with the heavenly community of the glorified ones who stand before God's throne and (even now!) declare that God's glory fills the entire earth (Isa. 6:3b). Indeed, in this praise all joy reaches its true fulfillment and destiny, for *"furiosa hominum laetitia, ubi sine Deo lasciviunt"* (Calvin on Ps. 96). All true joy draws upon this eschatological certainty about the kingdom. Melancholy is the sin *"instar omnium"* (Kierkegaard). A sermon on Psalm 96 must, if it is to be faithful to its text, under all circumstances bear some witness to the great joy that pervades it and, by means of a correct definition of its nature, aid the congregation in achieving this expression of faith that has become foreign to the church to such a large extent.

On the second point: With this its enlightenment the community stands very much alone. Those who know nothing of it are an overwhelming majority. *"Verus enim Deus in Judaea, quasi in obscuro recessu latebat"* (Calvin), hence the worldwide vocation of the community. In the first place, it has to proclaim the first commandment. Verse 5 thus speaks very broadly of "all gods." On the one hand it presupposes that the Gentiles have gods. Actually the Gentiles are continually engaged in the production and proclamation of gods. No nation survives in the world without gods. Thus there is only one option: gods or the living God. And now it is said that these gods are all "nothings." Thus there is no need even of a careful investigation; one actually does not need a closer acquaintance with these gods. "The world's secret is the nonexistence of its gods" (Karl Barth, *God in Action*, trans. E. G. Homrighausen and Karl J. Ernst [Manhasset, N.Y.: Round Table Press, 1963], p. 28). To worship gods means to deny God an honor rightly his alone; he is the sole creator, he and not the immanent mysteries to which man is constantly attributing the dignity of creator. Hence to know and to act accordingly is called "giving God the glory" (vs. 7).

There is nothing surprising in the fact that a nation that is little or not at all concerned with its larger environment clings to its God. But this look outward into the tumult of the religions and this triumphantly intolerant claim alone to know the Creator and Lord of all peoples—this is unique even in the history of religions. Israel did not, as most nations did, religiously encapsulate itself and wrap itself in its myth; it had precise knowledge about the phenomenon of the nations, of world history, and of the other religions, and it knew about the forces that are in motion in this field. Moreover, it believed in its worldwide calling. May the Christian community always have the good conscience that allows it also to see therein its own reflection!

The world, over which God has assumed his kingly rule, "shall not be moved" (vs. 10). It is the sturdy Old Testament immanent will of God that is attested here: God will not liquidate his creation. At the same time, this verse speaks of the duration and unshakable character of this kingdom; it has no part in the restless play of the *translatio imperii* exhibited by world history.

In verses 11-12 (cf. Ps. 98:7-8), joy of the nonhuman part of creation also is claimed, for now the world as creation once again comes into a right relationship with God and returns to his hands. In this connection Calvin refers to Romans 8:22. That is now a certainty because God has come into the world (the twofold emphatic *ba* in vs. 13 is in the perfect tense, as is the *malak* in vs. 10). While the psalm says that this coming of God is a coming in judgment, still this is not so much to be thought of as a punitive judgment; for *shaphat* means rather a "settling," a "helping one to gain one's rights." The positive predicates in verses 10b and 13b show how this judging is something of a helping and saving kind: "equity," "righteousness" (meaning loyalty), and "truth." Injustice and oppression will disappear from the world of nations.

81

Isaiah 40:3-8

Second Sunday in Advent

The text consists of two parts, each with its own similarly constructed introduction; the two are clearly separated by the concluding formula in verse 5b. The introduction to the first section reads "Listen, [a voice] is calling," and that to the second, "Listen, [a voice] is speaking." (In vs. 3 we must depart from Luther's translation. One can indeed also translate it as "the voice of one crying"—although the *kol* is better taken as a summons in the sense of "listen!"—but in any case the "in the wilderness" is to be connected with what follows: "In the wilderness prepare the way for the Lord!")

For the understanding of the first section four questions are to be explained and answered: (1) Who is calling? (2) Who is being called? (3) What is this "way"? and (4) Whence is the Lord coming along this way? We deal with these questions briefly in reverse order.

It is true that God's coming concerns the whole world ("all flesh," vs. 5), but it is clear that the prophet's idea is that God becomes manifest to the world through the world's perceiving his coming to his community (cf. 40:9-10). This community lives uprooted, without home, without hope, and without God. But God is coming to it; he is coming through the desert but along a road that must first be prepared. Obviously the first thought is of a processional avenue; religions everywhere celebrate the coming of the deity in cultic processions. But the impression of a processional avenue is immediately dispelled. The prophet is speaking of a way nowhere else taken by any god— through the desert! (The prophet in this case certainly is

82

thinking of the desert that lies between the community in exile and the Holy Land.) In order to lay this road oversize hindrances must be removed, mountains must be leveled, and valleys must be filled in! No, that is no ordinary processional avenue; it is a miracle road, no less. Who can be called upon to build it? Israel, who would first come into consideration, sits helpless in captivity. Men cannot do it at all; they would have to perform miracles. Celestial beings are summoned to build this road; and the one who calls them is also one of the lofty ones, something of a prince of angels. (There is a similar commissioning of one celestial being by another in Zech. 2:1 ff.)

Thus the content of the first section is presented as follows: the community sits in misery, but the prophet hears that in the heavenly realm things are stirring; there preparations are being made for God's coming to his own people in the world. God is coming to bring them home, and the exodus from the wretchedness of the exile will be analogous to and yet different from—more joyous than!— the exodus from Egypt (Isa. 52:11 ff.).

The sermon will have to be concerned with giving us a more comprehensive presentation of the word of God's coming and his marvelous way than is done in the verse of a hymn about preparing a way for God in our hearts. (This special meaning is indeed included in the total idea of God's coming.) What is involved is God's coming to his community, to the whole world. His coming is through the desert, through obstacles that can be eliminated only by miracle. On earth nothing of this is yet discernible; the community sits in misery; but above, in God's presence, everything is in motion; all the preparations for the coming of his kingdom are already made. Has not God built a way through the desert to us in Jesus Christ? A desert of insuperable hindrances lies between the celestial glory of God and the stable in Bethlehem. Indeed, God's way through the community of the Old Testament to Christ was also a way through the desert. And the way of Christ in his community until his glorification in the presence of the world also is a way through the desert. Calvin (in *Corpus Reformatorum*, LXV, 8) interprets the obstacles spiritually: they are the "depravity of our nature and the rebelliousness of our hearts."

We come to the second part: "Listen, [a voice] is speaking." (The celestial dimensions demanded a "call"; there the prophet was only a witness to what was going on above the earth; here now he is being addressed personally.) This now is the actual call to the prophetic office. The voice that falls on the prophet's ear is indeed here also an angel's voice. The question ("What shall I preach?") is exemplary in its appropriateness, for without a message given ad hoc by God there is no possibility of preaching. All sorts of considerations to stir the soul might readily have offered themselves to the prophet in the situation in which he and his community found themselves. Indeed, the prophet appears not to recognize as a "proclamation" even a repetition and reproduction of the rich religious tradition of his people. (And how often in our churches what happens is nothing but that!) He must personally receive a word spoken to him by God.

The message is at first radically destructive ("for the utter annihilation of the glorying in the flesh" [Calvin, in *ibid.*, p. 12]). Was the message of total perishability new to the prophet's hearers? Perhaps not entirely so (cf. Ps. 39, for example); and yet they will hardly have drawn on this awareness for their lives, continuing instead to be oriented to human hopes. But what certainly was new was what the prophet discloses as the cause of this bitter fate of all creatures: it is God himself! (Ps. 90:7-8 as a "nation's lamentation" has in mind rather a current distressful situation, and even Gen. 3:17 ff. does not actually deal

84

directly with imposition of the fate of death). The prophet speaks figuratively; *ruach* here has the sense of "wind," or "storm"; what is meant is God's burning wind, the dreaded sirocco that scorches all vegetation. In Palestine, vegetation dies under much more harsh circumstances than in our own setting. Its fate is sealed when the first east wind comes after the late rains. Hence this word about dying is very hard and does not admit of any softening interpretation. The true reality of death is hidden from the natural man, and precisely for the thoughtful man to hear of it is highly offensive. After all, what is involved is the "beauty," the "attractiveness," of man! (Perhaps *chasdo* should be emended to read *chemdo*.)

The sentence "The nation is grass" probably is a later addition; but what preacher today would dare to pass over this particular sharpening and later focusing of the message in a currently pertinent way?

The only thing that abides in the midst of all this susceptibility to death is the "word of our God." And this likewise should not be too quickly taken as internal; the primary meaning is not the word that is spoken to man's ear and heart. Instead, the prophet is thinking of the word uttered by God, thrust into history and into the world; and it is this word alone that is effectual and creative in history. The prologue of the prophetic book Isaiah 40-55—and our present text is to be understood in this sense—is to be interpreted from the perspective of the epilogue in Isaiah 55:10ff. As the rain and snow coming down from heaven "fructify" the earth, so also does God's word have a creative effect. And within a vast domain of death, this that is wrought by the word is the only thing that guarantees stability and deliverance. The message is enigmatic: humanity and all its works are hopeless and abandoned to death, but the word spoken by the prophet produces something that lasts. "Here the whole of the gospel is

85

summed up in a few words" (Calvin, in *ibid.*). In the context of Old Testament Israel, this divine word that is repeatedly thrust into history by the prophets also again and again effects judgment or preservation (in the form of historical facts). Moreover, it gives to the course of the history of this nation its direction, its purposeful progress toward Christ. When the time was fulfilled, the Word became flesh.

Peter, "the best interpreter of this passage" (Calvin, in *ibid.*, p. 13), has connected (I Peter 1:23-24) the message of the creative word of God to the grace of regeneration that is wrought in us.

Isaiah 52:13–53:12
Good Friday

The prophetic word about the vicarious death of the servant of God is a liturgical composition. In the prologue (52:13-15) and in the epilogue (53:11b-12) God himself is speaking; in the lengthier middle portion the community speaks (not the Gentiles!). The text is by no means especially corrupt. The clarity of the content of the utterances is another matter. The whole obviously is deliberately obscure and mysterious; many of the expressions remain uncertain and, in keeping with the mysterious style of the whole passage, cannot be made entirely precise and sharply focused.

About textual matters: in 52:13, *yaskil* is meant in the sense of "have success," "carry through successfully." In verse 14, instead of *'aleka* read *'alaw* ("over him"). In verse 15, *yazzeh* hardly means "sprinkle"; one would expect a contrast to *sham*^{e}*mu* ("to be rigid"), thus: "he shall cause to open up." In 53:1, *'al mi* could mean "about what kind" (thus referring to the servant), but it is more probably "about whom" (referring to the hearer). In verse 2, instead of *l*^{e}*phanaw* read *l*^{e}*phanenu* ("before us"). In verse 8, *dor* probably means "abode, place of residence," thus "and his abode, who considers it any longer?" Instead of *nega' lamo* read *y*^{e}*nugga' lammaweth* ("he was smitten to death"). In verse 10 Luther more correctly assumes a *yasim* instead of *tasim*. In verse 11, the Septuagint is to be followed by inserting *'or* after *yir'eh* (thus "he shall behold light").

Of greatest importance for any exposition is the fact that the divine utterance begins with the end, that is, with the exaltation and glorification of the servant of God before all the world. All that happens here clearly can be comprehended only from the perspective of its divine *telos*. It is only from the event of the glorification that the crucial light falls upon what has preceded it. At the same time, the divine prologue indicates the framework, the relationships, into which the servant of God is set. It will concern humankind, all peoples, and in particular their rulers; indeed, it will even strike them speechless. God already regards the glorification of his servant as accomplished and the world as already having been conquered by him. From the prophet's standpoint, however, this event is still in the future. Hence our text specifically stands between the suffering that belongs to the past and the exaltation that is to be anticipated. This explains the difficulties and afflictions that beset faith. Outwardly the community is confronted with the inability to believe. Everywhere in the Old Testament "the arm of the Lord" (53:1) is a reference to God's might. That now is the great expectation: here God has prevailed and triumphed; in this one person God is speaking and dealing with humanity. Here God becomes manifest, but here man also becomes manifest.

But who can believe all that? This perplexed question of verse 1 as a deep sigh about the fruitlessness of the preaching of the servant of God belongs to a true Good Friday sermon more than any sentimental mood. "We want to sigh and lament with the prophet and feel it as a kind of crucifixion when we see that our labor bears so little fruit, and we want to bring our lament before God. Such a sentiment is becoming in devout preachers who desire faithfully to do their work. Thus Isaiah explains that only a few will surrender to the gospel of Christ. The cry, 'Who believes what is preached?' means to say that out of a hundred who hear the gospel, hardly one will come to faith. The prophet, moreover, is not speaking for himself alone, but in the name of all preachers. Hence even though God should provide a number of ministers of the Word, still only a few would submit to their preaching. What will happen if these servants fail? . . . These words stand in opposition to the view that it is everyman's business to believe at will" (Calvin).

But even the community itself hardly knows how it came to believe, it is still so close to its own error and to its lack of understanding of what happened with the servant of God. The uses of the perfect tense in verse 3 signify something that has been overcome and yet continues to have the capability of becoming actual once again. But, as was said, while the community struggles with the assaults that beset it, God is already beholding the glorification of his servant before the world!

The stylistic form of the song in 53:1 ff. perhaps is that of the funeral dirge, which in other places is an attempt to draw up something of a summary of the earthly life that has ended. Thus the utterance of the community only begins when everything is already over and done. Now one can only look back and marvel—about him, about itself, and about others! In this sense there is no contemporaneity. As contemporaries they were not equal to the task; no one could watch with him. To a certain degree he was solitary, in comparison with whom all our experiences of solitude are indeed social; and in his solitude he was not even accompanied by the faith of his intimates. A Good Friday sermon will have to keep in view this limitation: even our faith really cannot comprehendingly follow the Lord on this his last journey or even walking in close company beside him unravel the mystery of what takes place. At best we can only subsequently comprehend what is said while looking back upon the completed events.

In the history of interpretation there is uncertainty about the more precise definition of the office of this one who suffers. Is he, as to his earthly function, a royal, a priestly, or a prophetic figure? It appears as though in this song all dignities have fallen away from him. If we say that he is no longer anything but a man, of course that too is misleading. The prophet calls him servant; he means the one who belongs entirely to God, but who therefore also is taken into God's confidence. He remained the man who is well pleasing to God (42:1), who in nothing lives for himself but entirely for the will of God. But from the standpoint of other men, this one who serves God so perfectly appears disfigured and marred, as one dying; in this fact man's nature and his distance from God become definitively clear.

The text does not permit us to look into the actual vicarious substitution. It is only proclaimed as having indubitably taken place. Indeed, the text cannot do enough to give repeatedly new expression to this very matter. While the church sees a twofold meaning concealed in the cross of Christ, a serving as God's representative and as man's representative, our biblical passage offers opportunity for emphasis on the latter: he who was wholly our own, the one who really was in solidarity with us—how monumentally is our fragmentation and the *incurvatio in semetipsum* outlined in verse 6!—he has gone forth and has taken upon himself the wrath of God. "This is a splendid antithesis: for in ourselves we are scattered, and in Christ brought together'' (Calvin).

He bore his sufferings differently from the way in which other men suffer. He did not perish in proud resistance. His death was neither a philosopher's nor a soldier's death (K. Heim); there was instead a readiness, an inmost acquiescence in his suffering (53:7). Our concepts of activity or passivity fail us in the face of this event: "It was a strange battle, when death and life wrestled." This is what faith in retrospect can repeat: here God's judgment upon us is taken seriously, and his holiness is satisfied before our eyes. In the man of sorrows who was stricken by God—though sinless (vs. 9b)—the true picture of humanity is held up before us. The punishment falls upon him, that we might have peace.

Every imaginable suffering obviously is heaped upon him. (The sufferings are not fully identifiable in detail. The picture that the prophet draws is hazy in this respect: destitution, repulsiveness, illness [leprosy?], loneliness, imprisonment, judicial penalties, sufferings of the soul.) But most of all, it is not clear from whom, humanly speaking, these sufferings are laid upon the servant of God. Those directly and (we would say) historically responsible for these sufferings are curiously ignored. We learn only by allusion (vs. 8b) that imprisonment and trial were involved. Who was responsible for all this? In this respect the prophet's word is in harmony with the sublime indifference of the gospel writers toward the question of the immediate and primary guilt for Jesus' death. At this point in our text there is something of a gap, which can be explained only by a lack of interest in this question. The only possible answer thrusts aside any other inquiry as inappropriate: the community that took an objective and nonparticipating stance in relation to this event, that did not at all concern itself with what had happened, now is smitten with the awareness that its sin was the cause of such afflictions.

With so sharp an accusation of detachment leveled against the community, one thing further must be all the more noticeable. The people and indeed even kings and nations stand round the servant; they praise and celebrate him. But they do not lift a finger to let themselves now be inspired by him to any similar action on their part. They do not interpret the unprecedented thing that they have witnessed (52:15) as a new ideal for life that they must imitate. They only accept from the hands of the servant of God the absolution—the new "righteousness" (vs. 11b) and reconciliation with God. It is as though they knew very precisely about the loneliness of this way of suffering and about Jesus' warning against any fanatical and reckless crossing-over of this boundary: John 13:36-38.

The epilogue lifts the significance of the event out of the intimacy of the community's conversation with itself and projects it on a worldwide scale: the many and the mighty (thus not merely the broken reed and the smouldering wick, 42:3) will be apportioned to him. On Christ's prize compare Ephesians 4:8 and Colossians 2:15.

Our meditation has been restricted to what is said in the Old Testament text. The preacher must decide for himself in each case to what extent his congregation expects him to touch upon the questions arising from the fact that this text was written 550 years before the birth of Christ. Did it originally refer to a historical fact, to the death of an unknown martyr, or to Deutero-Isaiah himself, from whom the preceding servant songs apparently stem? But what is predicated of the servant of God in Isaiah 53 transcends anything that could be said of a historical figure. Or is the text meant to be understood, even beginning with the prophet himself, as prediction (in spite of the striking assertions put in the perfect tense)? None of the many

91

scholarly attempts at explanation here is satisfactory. We are confronted with an enigma.

Isaiah 61:1-3, 10-11

Second Sunday After Epiphany

Interpretation of the text in terms of its historical setting is difficult because we know neither who the prophet is who is speaking here (Trito-Isaiah) nor the situation in the community that he is addressing. The only thing that is certain is that he was heavily dependent upon Deutero-Isaiah; indeed, his proclamation is precisely an updating of an earlier proclamation for a somewhat altered situation (the connection of our text with the servant songs has long been noted). For this reason Trito-Isaiah's activity usually has been placed in the early postexilic period, that is, in the time of the first settlement and rebuilding in the old homeland.

The text has a liturgical form: the word of promise in verses 1-9, attested and confirmed by the reference to the unique charismatic authorization of the prophet, is followed in verses 10-11 by the praise of the community as a response. But about the proposed omission of verses 4-9 from the sermon text the preacher must make a personal decision. The picture of the future is in fact historically immanent in the fullest sense and, as many expositors have emphasized, contains ideas which in the light of the New Testament can no longer be realized. Actually the Old Testament has never become currently pertinent for the Christian community except in an eclectic way. On the other hand, such an abrupt excision of a part of a text still is a serious business. Even here to interpret would be better than to eliminate (everything is concentrated on the idea of the glorification of the hitherto dishonored community). Above all, we should take care that in our zeal for rejecting such a form of immanently retributive divine justice we do not end up prescribing what God can and cannot grant. Our passage has in common with all prophetic perspectives on the future of radically different new orders this historically immanent aspect, and for this reason one may safely reckon on the possibility that what is proclaimed here also stands under a judging word—somewhat like that of Luke 9:55. But is not this judgment, wherever it is in place, much more safely—one could almost say more evidently—achieved in the act of a Christian proclamation without our making so much fuss about it or even denying an entire passage the possibility of speaking to us moderns? It is not on the contrary more important for our Christianity, so heavily oriented to what is inward, to acquire a new assurance that even here in this life things can once again be put in order by God? As we shall see in a moment, our text itself tends so strongly toward spiritualizing and internalizing that the interpreter must be especially careful not to let himself thereby be led away entirely from the great realities of which the text also speaks. And, finally, it should disturb us that the apostles saw the "incompleteness" of the Old Testament in an area altogether different from that in which it strikes the modern expositor.

According to all that we know of prophetic categories, what is said in verses 1ff. can only be understood as a prophet's testimony about himself. It cannot be determined with certainty whether Trito-Isaiah is claiming for himself all these vast powers, or whether he is rather putting them in the mouth of someone who is to come. The idea of an anointing is to be understood figuratively (as in I Kings 19:15-16), for in Israel only kings and priests were anointed. The task for which the prophet is empowered by being anointed now is unfolded in various aspects: to bring good news to those who are oppressed (the Septuagint renders this as *euangelisasthai*), to bind up the "broken-hearted," and "to proclaim liberty to the captives and the opening of the prison to those who are bound" (vs. 1 RSV). With "the year of the Lord's favor" (vs. 2 RSV) the prophet refers to the ancient sacral arrangement of the sabbath year or the year of jubilee (Lev. 25); for the concept of "liberation" also refers to an actual legal provision (cf. Jer. 34:8 ff.). "The year of the Lord's favor" then would mean that in that year an original property right belonging to God will become visibly manifest. The regulation about the year of jubilee governs the reversion of all property to the original owner after the passing of seven sabbath years; at this time also every person was to "return to his own family," i.e., to be set free from any sort of servitude for debts. Here also in certain circumstances the "redeemer" (*goel*) performed his function; he was the nearest kinsman and had to stand good for all his brother's obligations. Thus our text also speaks—at least implicitly—of the certainty, also expressed elsewhere in the Old Testament, that God is the real redeemer of men, their nearest kinsman, as it were, who will intervene on their behalf (Exod. 6:6; Isa. 41:14; 43:1; *et passim*). But what is novel and surprising about our prophetic text is that it perceives in the ancient sacral arrangement of the year of liberation a reference to a final eschatological act of deliverance, and thus it actualizes the priestly law in an entirely new fashion. The main idea of the year of liberation, restoration to the original situation, has been preserved; but now it is God himself who in a unique redemptive act once again reclaims entirely for himself all those who have fallen into the possession of other powers. H. Vogel (*Freijahr Gottes*, Berlin, 1949) not only has made the idea of God's year of liberation the central point of a sermon on Isaiah 61, but he has chosen it as the title of an entire collection of sermons. In the quotation in Luke 4:18-19, the reference to the "day of vengeance" is missing. Far-reaching theological conclusions are hardly to be drawn from that fact, though perhaps one may infer that Jesus had less reason to speak to his contemporaries about God's wrath against all transgressors of his commandments than is the case in the present situation. But especially worthy of note in the Old Testament is the disproportionate lengths of time signified by "year" and "day" (on this cf. Exod. 20:5-6). Thus the message is almost exclusively one of blessing and salvation. Its distinctiveness lies in the fact that in it God very personally inclines himself to the individual sufferer, for the earlier prophets admittedly spoke much more to the nation as a whole than to individuals. The abundant use of figurative language suggests that the prophet with his message is addressing the inward situation of the sufferers rather than their specific outward distresses. In this connection it would be rewarding to give the central position to the remarkable saying about the "brokenhearted" (nishbere leb), which appears also (with only minor variations) in Psalms 34:19; 51:19; and 147:3. The brokenhearted are people who are seized with a deep despair about themselves. This brokenness of their natural confidence in life and self is in the final analysis always a religious phenomenon, a state of being profoundly troubled and desolate in relation to God and precisely for that reason—according to biblical and Protestant theology—the sign of God's special nearness. Here is a wide-open field for a preacher who knows himself and his congregation. In verse 3 these suffering ones are called (in a somewhat awkward fashion textually) "Zion's weepers," which can also be understood to mean those who are weeping over Zion, that is, those who have taken to their own hearts the

95

sufferings of the people of God, their injuries and reverses. Thus it would mean all those unknown persons who are "grieved over Joseph's injuries" (Amos 6:6); but, further, the glad tidings are addressed to all those humble folk who are unable to secure any standing for themselves, and indeed, strange to say, do not even desire it: God knows about them. In order to give expression to the mystery of their belonging to God, still hidden but soon to be made manifest, the prophet seizes upon some expressions that even to the ears of his contemporaries had something of a bold sound: for example, "oaks of salvation" (in Deutero-Isaiah the word *tsedeqa* had the meaning of "salvation") and "planting of the Lord." Here the preacher will hardly be able to find corresponding expressions that will speak so directly to the heart as we must assume those did. The expression about the planting includes, in fact, the idea of a long drawn-out careful working. Thus the divine gardener has cultivated those who now appear to stand entirely in the shadows. Is there not a great deal of good that can be said about this marvelous planting of God, in which of course those who are thus cared for generally know nothing about the eyes of God that rest upon them in loving concern, and about the fact that in view of their abundantly demonstrated patience and submission they may be called, even now, a "planting for the glorifying of the Lord"?

While the message in verses 1-3 is concerned with persons, in the section composed of verses 4-9 (originally omitted in the proposed reading) the chief concern is with the change in external circumstances. Here the preacher at least should not overlook the passage in verse 4 about the rebuilding of ancient ruins. How much may an experienced pastor have to say about such ruins within the life of the congregation, of ground that has been lost by God's word in the course of the years, of all the good and necessary that he himself has already silently written off! Is it not always true

96

that the person inquiring about the work of God first sees what is negative—that is, loss, betrayal, exhaustion, and boundless frustration and denial? It is precisely this little faith that the prophet is opposing. But a rebuilding of the ruins that is actually well pleasing to God also involves an utterly unsentimental demolition of many false facades, many wrong and unauthentic conceptions of God, of his church, and of his word. Such a rebuilding would be something entirely different from a religious and churchly restoration.

Perhaps never in the course of its history has the church been so urgently summoned to turn its face toward the world as now. It is to rebuild the ruins, and it should do this in a literal as well as in a figurative sense. It is to help people in body and soul, with deeds or with admonition, instruction, and counsel. Under some circumstances these could be very worldly deeds and instructions, but they must issue from the gospel. If this is done, the church may and must also be able to speak in altogether practical and political fashion, and cast its vote in matters of politics, economics, or the life of the nation in general. The people of God, who live in praise of their Lord, who are filled with a joy that nothing can take from them, not even the horrors of recent years and the dreadful distresses of the present, cannot keep silent when all around the people are perishing in body and soul before the gates of the holy city, hardened in fatalism, in nihilism disintegrating in hatred and bitterness, and in ruthless battles against each other are destroying themselves. (G. Dehn in a meditation on our text: "Herr, tue meine Lippen auf," V [1948], 58)

In verse 8b is sounded the conception of a new covenant which God will conclude with his people. One consequence of this will be that the people of God "will be known among the nations." There will be something about this people that will be distinctive, something by which others will "recognize" them (ancient interpreters thought here of something like a positive counterpart to the mark of

Cain). This is first addressed to the humbled and despised position of the people of God in the world of nations. But in this connection the preacher will also think of the voluntary incognito into which so many Christians like to retreat—out of a religious shyness.

Verses 10-11 now contain—as in a liturgical event—the answer, the echo to the message that has been given (in this respect comparable to the Magnificat in Luke 1:46 ff., with which it actually has a certain similarity). The crucial test for the sermon that is delivered now will be whether the congregation can sincerely repeat at least something of these words of thanksgiving, even though perhaps not in such full tones, but more soberly and with more reserve. The salvation event that comes to the community and to the individual is set forth here as God's act of clothing them anew, an act in which God himself covers what would be man's shame. Thus God has already taken the first men under his protection by clothing their shame (Gen. 3:21). But how joyless, depressed, and disconcerted are Christians in a world over which God's year of liberation is already announced!

A sermon on such an Old Testament text can be justified only if the preacher is convinced that in the ancient word of the prophet something is said to him about Jesus Christ, something that is given to him in no other passage in the Bible and that is not interchangeable with other texts. To put it briefly, he must be persuaded that he has a commission to fulfill here. When he reaches for this Old Testament text, he must not think that he is doing something somehow superfluous, since for the fulfillment of this commission New Testament texts appear to be more obviously suited. Such a roundabout approach to Christ by way of the Old Testament in a rather rhetorical and ornamental manner could never be justified. The decision on this question is only apparently made easier by the fact that according to Luke 4, Jesus applied this text to himself in the synagogue at Nazareth. Even someone who assumes that there we are dealing with actual words of the historical Jesus (indeed, precisely a person with such an assumption!) must pose the question whether the Christ event in that case must still be made comprehensible for the church of today by such a reference to the ancient book. And if so, why does he then preach on Isaiah 61 and not directly on Luke 4:14ff.? Thus the decision cannot possibly be based exclusively on Luke 4; it must be set on a much broader plane—namely that almost the entire New Testament introduces Christ into the most widely diverse Old Testament texts in order to "fulfill" (or "judge") them. Thus the decision is based on the fact that all these texts—in this way or that, but mostly this way!—have a unique connection with Christ and that they therefore are adduced by the authors of the New Testament, little by little, for the purpose of interpreting and making understandable the Christ event.

Jeremiah 29:4-14

The letter of Jeremiah to the exiles in Babylon—the first pastoral epistle of the Bible—was written between the first and second deportations (597 and 586 B.C.). As the detailed introduction shows, it was sent by the hand of a delegation who had been sent to the great King Nebuchadnezzar on some mission. Beginning at verse 15, the text manifestly lacks the splendid rational compactness of its beginning. The second part of the epistle apparently is not free from interpolations (cf. Jer. 24:8-10; 25:4). Verse 15 is only a torso, and verses 16-20 are not found in the Septuagint. Hence it is justifiable for the preacher to confine himself to the exposition of verses 3-14.

On the text: The *yether* in verse 1, "the rest . . . ," is not clear; its omission from the Septuagint, however, is a later smoothing of the text. In verse 7 perhaps we should read, with the Septuagint, *ha'arets* ("of the land") instead of *ha'ir* ("of the city"). In verses 12-14 the text, which up to this point certainly is in good shape, has obviously fallen into disorder. Instead of the very dubious *halaktem* in verse 12, we should likely read, following the Targum, *'anitikem* ("I will answer you"). The conclusion of verse 13b is in verse 14a: "I will be found by you." Thus there are four pairs of concepts: call—answer; pray—hear; seek—find; inquire after—be found.

The epistle allows us to discern in unmistakably clear terms the inward frame of mind of the recipients. Uprooted from all familiar circumstances by the barbaric deportation, they found themselves on the one hand suffering a kind of paralysis in relation to their environment and their immediate tasks and on the other hand indulging in passionate political hopes: things could not remain in this way, for God's own honor and trustworthiness now are at stake! But as wide a range of possibilities as there were for the currents moving in their souls, still it obviously was far from their minds to understand this their present situation as any of God's doing.

In this unrest of unbelieving dejection and of hope equally devoid of faith, the voice of the prophet breathes a realism and a soberness that could put any politician to shame. What concerns the prophet is, first of all (simply and altogether without fanaticism), to involve in the present those people who, captured by despair, gazed into the past or those who, in excited appetites for something sensational, expected of the future some political or

100

perhaps even apocalyptic upheavals on a grand scale. Ahead of all else there stands the commandment to take the present seriously as a divine dispensation. It is significant to note how three times in our text the deportation is emphasized as caused by God directly ("whom I have sent into exile"[vss. 4, 7 ,14]) and thus not merely "permitted."

Carefully, step by step, Jeremiah leads his readers to the validity and the duration of this their present: in the Orient houses are quickly built, though more time is required for the planting of gardens; but to marry off children and to think of grandchildren! How objective here is the summons to simple involvement in society, against a fanaticism that believes that this interim situation does not at all deserve to be taken seriously!

But in the prophetic admonition there is much more than the matter of involving the recipients in this present time that is under God's dispensation. For the first time in the history of the people of God on earth the community was thrust out into the alien situation in the world and was consequently captured by a doctrine which even yet the church of Christ has not escaped. Previously the entire communal life, as well as the individual life, was bound to the cultus. Israel lived on holy soil; all functions of life occurred under the shadow of sacral signs and were nourished by sacral powers that radiated outward from the cultic center of the temple through all areas of life to the boundaries of death. The deported people were snatched overnight out of this cluster of protective sacral orders. Now they lived in an "unclean land" (I Sam. 26:19; Amos 7:17; Ezek. 9:1ff.), and it is impossible for us to over-estimate the force of the question that this presents to them. In view of this background, Jeremiah's directions are amazing; they contain a justification of what is secular, worldly; indeed, they propose to offer encouragement to what is worldly. It is from this perspective that all the specific directions that Jeremiah gives acquire their specific sharpness, of which the preacher must be conscious—even the passage about the marriage of the children! For even for this directive a good conscience had to be provided for those distant exiles. An authorization, an ordinance had to be given. Of course the sentences have such an unromantic sound that the modern reader will hardly be able to detect in them what he thinks of in relation to love and marriage.

Of special import is verse 7, which offers guidance for the relationship of the community to her environment. This world—which certainly was not very kindly disposed toward the community, but which also had such great and different concerns—from this her environment the community might not detach herself; she had an obligation to pray for it. This is not "already" the commandment of love for one's enemies, as many expositors have gloried in believing. Here the prophet is concerned simply with the community, that is, that she will find the right relationship with her larger environment, that she will share in bearing the world's concerns and will remain in solidarity with the world. It has pleased God to connect the well-being of his community with that of the world at large, and since the world supports the community—albeit unwittingly and under the divine commission—the community should also be ready to serve the world as well. This is a wide-open field for the preacher, who is sensitive to the mortal danger of that wicked superspiritual standing aloof to which the church of Christ is vulnerable.

With all of this, one might say, Jeremiah is reproving homesickness, that is, the homesickness that looks backward as well as forward; he is speaking against that dissatisfaction, that age-old human will to revolt that can wear so many different garbs. Jeremiah presupposes this homesickness, but he does not arouse it further. Instead he says: "Build houses, plant gardens!" This constitutes the great difference between him and the dreamers who still had the function of sanctifying this homesickness and then quieting it. (It is significant that he uses the Hiphil word *machlemim*, which shows how those dreamers practice a kind of influence over the people in what they dream!)

Now the thoughtful hearer of course will want to be sure that in all this he is not being offered a highly irrational and unspiritual philistinism. And, further, is this not being directed once again along a way where sooner or later he will suffer exploitation and the plundering of his last farthing by the world? Now in verses 10-11 Jeremiah speaks of what lies beyond these houses and gardens. This entire situation of building and planting and of praying for Babylon—in spite of its current validity—will last only for a period to which God has set limits. The "seventy years" are not to be understood as a period of time that can be calculated in the history of men, but as a round number, a general, longer period of time, "a period of world history" (Volz). Jeremiah allots seventy years to the Neo-Babylonian kingdom. Thus this does not have to do with the prediction of the length of the exile. (The beginning point from which Jeremiah makes his calculation is uncertain; perhaps from Nebuchadnezzar's assumption of the throne in 605 and perhaps from the fall of Nineveh in 612.) The figure is approximately correct—the fall of Babylon came in 538—but it by no means needs to be regarded as a *vaticinium ex eventu*; again, it is too imprecise for that.

Hence Jeremiah is able to preach against that homesickness because this entire experience of exile has its limits set by God. It is set, so to speak, within large brackets, and God's paternal intentions of salvation stand before and above and around this bracketed period. "I know the plans I have for you" (RSV) is to be interpreted in the sense of Jeremiah 1:12: God has not forgotten his saving intention; he is watching over his word even where everything seems to argue to the contrary. On the "good word" compare Jeremiah 24. In verse 11 Jeremiah refers to the dawning of deliverance only in a general way with the two nouns *acharith* ("end," used here probably in the sense of "future"; cf. Jer. 31:17; Prov. 23:18; 24:14; Ps. 37:37) and *tiqvah* ("hope"), which is generally understood as a *hendiadys*, "hopeful future" (Giesebrecht); Luther's translation, "a future for which you hope," is more graceful and probably equally correct. In verse 14 similarly general terms are used to speak of the "change" that God will effect. The expression *shubh sh^ebuth,* a favorite of Jeremiah's, probably is not derived from *shabah* ("captivity") but from *shubh* and means "turn, change, reversal." Who wants to decide whether the passage that follows this in verse 14 is "a later addition with set formularies"? ("Jeremiah in his letter is writing for the present the very opposite of what is" [Volz].) It is true that the comfort he offers proceeds in exactly the opposite way from the usual mode of comfort: he does not begin with a reference to the great time that is coming, and he does not exhort his readers to look away from the here and now. Only at the last, after he has demolished the foolish human expectations, does he speak of the salvation that God is going to achieve. Of still more significant import is the fact that this sentence appears to presuppose the Diaspora in the entire world (Rudolph).

We have spoken of the all-pervading secularity into which the community has been thrust for a while; yet in this existence that is essentially devoid of the cultus one thing still is possible, and that is prayer. And here Jeremiah is speaking specifically of a serious concern about God as well as a precondition for finding God, indeed—according to the present form of verse 14—a precondition even for being saved at all.

What would have come of this experience in exile without the prophets? An age that because of any sort of disruption in its tradition no longer is conscious of any binding obligations placed upon it cannot of itself find the proper norms even for the most elementary actions. But here in Jeremiah's letter is that authorization for the simplest kind of reconstruction, for a life that in spite of all the secularity must not be lived out either in resignation or in fanaticism because God's intentions of salvation stand above that life. Is this not the kernel of the entire doctrine of justification? (The commentaries rightly point also to I Thess. 4:11-12 and II Thess. 3:10 ff.) We learn from Jeremiah 29:24-25 something of the aftereffect that the letter had.

Although in principle no Old Testament text is made to refer to the Christian church without a certain refraction of its meaning, a certain metamorphosis (after all, we are not Israel with its cultus, with the anticipation of an immanent salvation, and so forth), still in this case the congregation will not expect of the preacher any theological explanations about the relationship of the Old Testament to the church of Christ. By virtue of its current relevance, this message of Jeremiah will quite by itself become "contemporary" for the church of today.

Jeremiah 31:31-34

First Sunday in Advent

The almost too familiar pericope about the new covenant stands in the so-called book of comfort for Ephraim, Jeremiah 30-31. Ephraim, the major part of the former Northern Kingdom, collapsed in the year 722 B.C. under the blows of the Assyrians. Its territory was incorporated into

105

the Assyrians' provincial system and was settled by heathen colonists (II Kings 17:24 ff.). Thereby it was, according to human judgment, handed over to death as a corporate entity; salvation history appeared to have come to a halt as far as Ephraim was concerned. Approximately one hundred years later, after the process of change and decay in the community had advanced without intermission, Jeremiah addressed to this territory, torn from Israel and therefore dead, a comprehensive message of salvation, the last part of which forms our pericope. "God promises that they shall once again be one body" (Calvin). Even this state of affairs should be considered from all angles by the interpreter, for the Christian community—precisely to the extent that it is obliged to recognize itself as such an Ephraim—may believe that such a thing in the old covenant happened as an example (a prototype) for us (I Cor. 10:11).

Ancient Israel was conscious of being in covenant with God. This was not a religious idea, but a very immediate and happy reality. Israel simply found itself in this relationship of nearness to God; in God's commandments a sovereign right of God over this nation was proclaimed; and a life of fellowship with God was offered to it. For according to the witness of the Old Testament, obedience to the commandments simply carried with it the promise of life (Deut. 30:15 ff.).

It is not necessary to emend the *baalti* in verse 32 ("even though I had become their Lord," or perhaps even "have wedded them"). Indeed, God "took them [i.e., the community of the old covenant] by the hand." This expression is strikingly tender and affectionate (like that of Hos. 11:1-4). It carries with it the idea of paternal guidance and patience: God has led the people of Israel, like children out of Egyptian bondage, through the pitfalls, perils, and afflictions of the wilderness-wandering into the freedom of the realm of his dominion. But *they* have broken the covenant (the *hemmah* stands in an emphatic position, before the verb: it was none of God's doing; cf. Mic. 6:3ff.). Thus the history of the old covenant actually exhibits something of a collapse of the divine plan of salvation: through its own fault Israel has foundered, has suffered shipwreck on God and his commandments.

The declaration that the covenant had been broken certainly was no exciting novelty to the prophet's hearers! To what extent it had been broken is not detailed here; the prophet assumes that the fact is self-evident. If one wanted an answer to this question, the response that the prophets give is quite clear and unequivocal: with the formation of a state (that is, after the period of the judges) Israel began to detach itself from the ancient patriarchal ordinances and orders. As a state with a king it began more and more to act by principles dictated by reasons of state; it began to allow itself to be guided in its political actions by tactical perspectives and in the military sphere to detach itself from the order of the "holy war" (horses and chariots!); and in its striving for political security it began to rely on earthly power factors (treaties) instead of upon God alone. In similar fashion Israel retreated to the territory of the internal orders of the divine commandments. With the formation of a state a great process of emancipation set in.

Thus this covenant of God with Israel was dissolved and annulled. But "after this time" God's grace intends to establish a new covenant. A covenant inaugurates a relationship of fellowship, a relationship that is based upon quite specific orders of life. So now the first question is about orders and structures of life that pertain to this new covenant. Obviously they are altogether the old ones; they are God's law. And how could they be anything else? God's holy will was not an arbitrary proposal, that is, one among many possibilities. And how could that will, solemnly

107

announced to man by God, be annulled and abolished? It is of crucial importance for the expositor to see clearly that the orders of life of the new covenant are precisely the same as those of the old one. "Thus we see that God had spoken thus from the very first; not even a syllable was later changed, insofar as it pertained to the summary of doctrine" (Calvin). (And that is one of the reasons the Christian church absolutely cannot surrender it!) But then what is new about this new covenant?

"I will put my law in their hearts."

What is new obviously is the way it is appropriated. In the old covenant God's will for men was written on tablets of stone. It came to man, who had fallen away from God, from without, as an alien will; and it had to bring him into judgment. Thus Israel said at Sinai: "Do not let God speak to us, lest we die" (Exod. 20:19). God will place his commandment in the heart and will of man, so that man bears God's will in his heart, united with his own will.

This passage has been the point of departure for classical misinterpretations. The contrast of "here outward obedience to the letter, and there inward attitudes" is utterly incorrect. Ancient Israel also knew that God's will is to be fulfilled with the whole heart, with all one's powers (Deut. 6:5). Even less correct, of course, is the point of all this as a sanctifying of the innermost soul, of the best in man, the naïve and immediate as the opposite pole to the law. "Feeling, conscience, a sense of what is good, the obscure compulsion of the man who is aware of the right way, the sensitivity of the soul for its task, the obligation that has become actuality, the personality that has directly and unconsciously become one with all that is good" (Niebergall). It is somewhat a different matter with the motto of pure idealism: "Receive the Deity into your will, and it will ascend from its worldly thrones" (Schiller, *Die Ideale*). Here there is not so easy a concession, and besides, there is

108

undoubtedly a connection, in terms of intellectual history, with the message of the gospel. But here there is a classic example of the transformation of the gospel into law. And is it then after all a possibility for man to proclaim as a universal truth this which God has promised to effect?

Behind this entire pericope there stands, unexpressed, the conviction that it lies beyond the powers of man to prepare himself for the fulfillment of God's will and to render himself virtuous (Jer. 13:23!). The initiative (indeed, all that is done) issues exclusively from God. What is involved here is a gift and not the result of any kind of human striving, even the loftiest and most devout striving. This event signifies (1) a total renewal of the relationship of man to God, and (2) is an eschatological event.

1. In opposition to the thousandfold attempts of man to gain a connection with God in some magical or mythic way, our prophetic word insists on man's submission in obedience to the divine will. But God himself will effect the perfect obedience that will ultimately bring man into harmony with his creator. He will himself—as we can also express it—create the new man. This will not happen through man's being equipped with marvelous powers and capacities or, at any rate, not through his being delivered from the distresses and limitations that now surround him. With a sublime one-sidedness, the renewal of the human heart is held to be fully sufficient for the healing of the broken relationship with God. It is precisely through the writing of God's commandment on man's heart that from the very depths of his being man wants nothing other than God's will to be done. Of course *leb* means more than our word "heart." According to the Old Testament understanding, it is not only the seat of feeling but also the seat of understanding and the very life of the will.

The precondition of this renewal from God's side is the forgiveness of sins. One could interpret our pericope in terms of Jeremiah 17:1: at present sin is deeply engraved in human hearts. Only when this inscription has been erased can God inscribe his own will there. The result of this renewal is the end of the teaching office.

The phrase "to know Yahweh" does not at all mean a knowledge of God in the speculative, intellectual sense. *Yadah* denotes rather "to experience, to become acquainted or familiar with." *Yodea* means "friend." Even the use of the verb to denote sexual intercourse between man and woman is by no means merely a euphemism. Thus it is rightly affirmed that an element of love is included in the word *yadah* (Procksch). Significant here is the preferred use of the concept of *daat Elohim* ("knowledge of God") in Hosea (2:22; 4:1, 6; 5:4; 6:3, 6; 3:4) as the essence of the proper renewed relationship of man to God. On this whole matter see the article on *ginosko* by Bultmann in the *Theological Dictionary of the New Testament*.

2. According to the prophet's testimony the new covenant is a gift of the end-time. It is fulfilled in Jesus Christ (Mark 14:24; Luke 22:20). Jesus Christ was the new man, and as the firstborn among many brethren he bore God's will fully and completely in his own will ("My food is to do the will of him who sent me" [John 4:34]). Insofar as we belong to Christ, the prophecy also pertains to us, insofar as we now have already "died" and "been raised" with him (Col. 3:1-3). This our new man is already present now by faith, but this our new life in Christ is still "hidden," just as the risen Lord is also still hidden in this present epoch of world history. Thus in a peculiar sense we now stand between the covenants, and all our advent expectation is grounded in this fact.

To the extent that our personal spiritual life is still subject to the flesh, we still have need of the teaching office. Yet even now this teaching office may no longer be legal in nature; it is steadily becoming more limited, for it

110

acknowledges the freedom of the Holy Spirit that likewise is bringing to maturity in relation to God every person under its instruction (II Cor. 1:24). Thus among Christians every teaching office is, as a matter of principle, always "ready to vanish away" (Heb. 8:13 RSV). If it were only taken more seriously, how much this assurance could do to quiet the sighs and groans of the theologians!

As has long been recognized, there is a kind of paraphrase of our text in Jeremiah 32:28-41. It should be utilized as a help in the task of exposition.

Haggai 2:1-9

Twenty-second Sunday After Trinity

The word of the prophet is uttered in the late autumn of the year 520 B.C. In the year 538 Cyrus had given the community of exiles his permission to return home. Thereupon many took advantage of the opportunity (though more than a few were unable to do so). Conditions in the homeland were very difficult. Where there was enthusiasm, it quickly subsided. In the period of the first reconstruction, the building of the temple has been postponed. This is when Haggai's first utterance is heard; he has a different answer to the question of priorities of obligations. How could the Israelites hope for blessing and prosperity when they have failed first to put their own relationship to God in order! ("Seek ye first the kingdom of God.") Thus the question of the rebuilding of the temple at that time became for the Old Testament community a matter of *status confessionis*. Thereupon the work was taken up. Our text begins a few weeks later. A great

111

despondency has seized the community; the little bit that has been done in the interim shows how poor the whole is going to be. Small faith makes comparisons with what was earlier and holds that which is to come in low regard! The prophetic word knows the future in entirely different terms: in a little while God will shake the world; the temple will emerge from its insignificance; and all nations will present their treasures to God and enter into his salvation. Here Haggai is working with a set of eschatological ideas that were traditional in Israel. In our pericope the motif of the eschatological unveiling of Zion is passed over, because it is presupposed that this idea is well known. Here our text is to be interpreted in terms of Isaiah 2:2ff.: Zion, heretofore hidden in the form of a servant, now manifest in glory (*doxa*) before all the world—this indeed is the presupposition of the nations' streaming together. Isaiah 60:1ff. is akin to this—only the application is to the postexilic situation. On the disunited feelings of the Old Testament community of that time with regard to the new temple that was in the making, compare especially Ezra 3:12-13! In verse 6 the '*od* '*achat m^e'at* is almost incapable of being translated and is hardly original here. It probably means "yet a little, and then." (Unclear also is the intended reference of the "once again." Is it the theophany at Sinai?)

The text shows the great distress and the great comfort of the community that is moving toward the eschaton. In the new covenant the existence of the Old Testament community is repeated as on a higher plane, because it, too, is moving toward a fulfillment; and what is said in this text about an unbelieving or a believing attitude with respect to the temple will apply in the new covenant with respect to the church. Furthermore, in all that concerns the church, weeping and rejoicing will always be intermingled, so that from a distance one cannot distinguish between them.

Weeping: The community is still only a remnant (vs. 2b);

it can look back on much more glorious times. The comparison is very obvious, and abundant use is made of it. The prophet addresses himself in pastoral fashion to the community's despondency; he himself "touches the most painful point" (Frey), the lowly and insignificant nature of the beginnings of the kingdom of God. If one calculates what can be done in the future in terms of what has already been achieved (by man) the result is discouraging. In response to all this the commands of the prophet are very urgent: "Be comforted!" "Fear not!" "Work!" The rightness and validity of such demands does not lie in a defiant human "nevertheless," but in the fact that God's Spirit is given to the community (vs. 5). The exhortation to work should be carefully distinguished, in the exposition, from the well-known misunderstandings of Protestant culture. On the contrary, care should be taken to impress upon the congregation that sublime grace that in the midst of work that is unrewarding and even accursed, there is actually a work in which God shares. Here we first may certainly hear a promise that is attached to the so often doubtful "church work" and also to every activity that, at the instigation of the Holy Spirit, sacrifices itself in faith or in love. It is God's good pleasure that we should build from below, so to speak, to meet the coming of his kingdom.

Rejoicing: The great shaking of the world of which the prophet speaks did not arrive with the coming of Christ. The heavenly guest entered our world quietly and inconspicuously. Thus even for us in our time that shaking of the world has not yet come, and it will happen when Christ emerges from his hiddenness in glory and assumes his rule. But the marvel that the prophet proclaims is that we already know, in the present, that which is future; here and now it can be the object of our work. "With this grand prospect the miserable work that the community is pursuing towers into the next age and therein acquires its significance and fulfillment" (Frey). Or, conversely, the next age towers into our world. It is not the cosmos alone, however, that is "shaken," but the nations as well (cf. Isa. 52:15: nations are "startled"). When the place where God heretofore has been doing his work in profound obscurity becomes manifest in glory, then the heathen will be inwardly vanquished. The bringing of their gifts, of course, is first of all a sign and a testimony of their reverence, their submission in obedience to the living God; but then, as verse 8 shows, it has a certain independent significance as well. In the eschaton God's sole sovereign right will prevail likewise with reference to the treasures of the nations. In the present world-epoch these treasures have a use that is only temporary; they have been withdrawn from their original and true destiny, which is to belong to God. But they too will return to the only rightful possessor. The concept of treasures (literally "the most precious possession of all the peoples") is a broad and inclusive one: it may be thought of as referring to all the values and arts in which the heathen take pleasure and which they deify. On his way to the cross Christ passed them by, and in this present world-epoch the church will also follow her Lord's example in this respect. But the church knows the provisional and temporary nature of the condition of being in exile, in which those treasures are found; she knows the Christ is also the lord and owner of those treasures; and she knows that the *regnum Christi* is wider than the church (cf. Matt. 2).

The *shalom* in verse 9b probably would better be translated as "salvation." The word also, and perhaps even primarily, carries the meaning of a state of eschatological peace among the nations (cf. especially Isa. 2:4), but in addition to that it embraces all spiritual and material blessing that God will bestow on those who turn obediently to him. And that is the spot which according to human

114

calculation appears so barren and devoid of all hope. But against all the assaults upon faith, the prophet urges an *active confession* of this still hidden salvation which God will make manifest in glory.

Malachi 4:1-6

Second Sunday in Advent

This pericope, as it is presently prescribed, on the one hand breaks apart a unit of prophetic discourse and on the other hand combines into a whole an originally independent unit (4:4-6) with what precedes it. The latter is more justifiable than the former. If the preacher does not choose to disregard the prescribed reading and to begin his text with 3:13—this is really advisable—he still must in one way or another incorporate into the sermon the essence of the passage that has been omitted (3:13-18).

I

In verses 13 ff. the prophetic utterance provides a clear picture of the internal situation of the community of that time. The community is not dead; indeed, one could not deny that it manifests a certain theological vitality. It is stirred by issues, and its members confer with one another; indeed, it is manifesting repentance, or at least it has imposed upon itself measures of abstinence (vs. 14b). But it offers the unedifying picture that at the same time it is casting sidelong glances, in dissatisfaction and in secret envy, at the good fortune of the godless; it asks, "What do I have to show for my piety?" In a word, it is a community that in its service to God and its waiting upon him has lost

115

its simplicity and naturalness and is beset by temptations; one that is a bit peevish and morose. The prophet makes it clear that this grumbling community that complains about God ("He is not the God he used to be") wearies God. God is simply enduring this community!

According to the original text, verse 16 has the following meaning: "Those who feared God talked with each other; but the Lord took note of it and heard it, and there was written before him a book of remembrance of those who fear the Lord and give attention to his name." Thus here begins the word of consolation, a consolation that must shame the community: while these people put their heads together to exchange expressions of dissatisfaction, in heaven books are being kept on everything! God witnesses every conversation on matters of faith! (Cf. Job 42:7.) Thus this prophetic saying deals with the hiddenness of God in this present world-epoch. Anyone who belongs to this God must constantly appear in the eyes of the world (and often enough in his own eyes as well) as a person whom God has forsaken (Ps. 22). But for their comfort the prophet proclaims that in heaven books are being kept on everything.

But the community should know, above all else, that the great and terrible "day of the Lord" is coming, that is, the day on which God will finally move into the center of things. Up until that day, the relation of men and things to God is, for the natural mind of man, the most remote and questionable among all the relationships in which men find themselves. Thus in the prophet's words God can describe this day as "the day when I act" (RSV). It is not as though God had not been guiding all things all along, but that his action will then become manifest to all the world. And this becoming manifest on God's part—an old and ever newly exciting theme of the prophets'! —will be for men a terrible surprise. Then of course even the community will become aware that the real issue is not its petty and personal claims, but God's own cause (Frey). Thus the sermon also would have the task of saying, to a generation that after severe and catastrophic events is now pressing with all its energies for reconstruction, something about the great and final collapse that awaits all human endeavors (cf. Jer. 45), a collapse the prophet, along with almost all the witnesses of the Old and New Testaments, sees as a consuming fire coming from God.

This day of the Lord will finally and decisively separate the haughty from those who fear God. Among all the innumerable varieties of human nature, this classification (in our present age so doubtful and often apparently inadequate) will demonstrate what is ultimate. On that day all the intermediate gradations which we men are accustomed to observing with such fine distinction will be lacking; instead, the only issue will be a simple basic decision for or against God. The prophet's viewing the fear of God as the mark of this fundamental decision becomes the sign of great grace: God will not look for any sort of great achievement that could be cited. And yet this must cause some disquiet to our present-day churches, for the fear of God has become to a considerable extent an alien idea even for so-called vital and vigorous churches. The haughty (or presumptuous) ones are those who scorn the will of God and who themselves arbitrarily prescribe everywhere the law governing their activity.

The images in which the eschatological event is illustrated are intermingled in a way that is esthetically awkward (fire that will consume root and branch, the rising sun of righteousness, calves that go forth leaping from the stall), and in part they tend to cancel each other out (this too is an indication of the great disruption!). This self-revelation of God to the world from which he was hidden will come to those who fear God as a sunrise over a

117

landscape that has lain for a long time in the cold and dark of night (cf. Rom. 13:11-12). The reception of salvation is set forth in an almost rough, crude picture as a going forth, a leaping of calves from the stall. It may be interpreted as an expression of a strong, vital joy over a great liberation. But it goes beyond the picture of a place over which the fire of judgment has raged and that is now covered with the ashes of the rebels (Frey). If we have here a prediction of participation in the final judgment, the passage must be interpreted in the light of I Corinthians 6:2 and Matthew 13:28. But the interpreter must also think of a restriction and warning in the sense of Luke 9:55.

There may be congregations in which no other word of the text is so attentively or perhaps even eagerly noted as that of the rising sun of righteousness or justice. But God's *justitia salutifera* brings something different from what is demanded by the call for socially compensatory justice. Precisely on the basis of our scriptural text a word can also be pronounced against that complaining and disputing with God. The rising of the sun of God's righteousness and justice may and should be a comfort to those who fear God, not to those who present God with an account of their claims.

II

According to Malachi's message, God will send in advance of this great *consummatio mundi* a messenger, the prophet Elijah. Jesus Christ has come, and he was more than Elijah! This is one of the passages in which it becomes evident how far in many respects the New Testament fulfillment has gone beyond the Old Testament promise. And, nevertheless, the community of the new covenant also is once again an expectant community; it awaits the return of the Lord and his glorification before the world and the establishment of the kingdom of God. Thus there is repeated in this community the existence of the Old Testament community, and Christ's community may see what Israel expected of Elijah being taken up and fulfilled by the greater offices of Christ.

The preacher in any congregation probably can anticipate the question of a messenger or, in impersonal terms (as it is often posed), of some variety of signs that could inform us about the date and hour on the great cosmic clock of history. Consciously or unconsciously today, all men are turning their ears to history and inquiring about any kind of indications by which they can at least find some orientation in the dread darkness (just as Isaiah is asked, as a sentinel, by a voice from Edom about the hour in history: "Watchman, is the night almost over?" [21:11]). In response to this yearning the preacher can only point to Jesus Christ, to his forerunners, and the signs of his return (Matt. 24); for other than these signs that God's grace has given in our nighttime, history, in the face of our queries, maintains a stony silence.

We are to note that the end will come "suddenly" (Mal. 3:1), and before this end the messenger will come. The community knows him and knows that upon his return he will complete the work that has been begun in the community. Of this work the prophet predicts only the internal peacemaking work in the Holy Spirit. The conflict between generations is regarded by Malachi simply as a symptom of the universal inner division among men. This division becomes most painfully evident in the circle of the closest family, that is, among those who are of the same flesh and blood. Genuine, unforced harmony, an authentic and free fellowship, is possible only in the Holy Spirit—among nations, within a nation, and in the circle of the family—here is a wide-open field for any preacher!

119

Today there are many inquiries about a suitable foundation for a life of human community and fellowship; but a life that is not founded upon obedience to the commandments of God must remain without promise. But a life that is lived in keeping with the divine ordinances has, according to the witness of both Testaments, the promise of blessing both temporal and eternal (I Tim. 4:8). Thus the community is to continue in faith to wait expectantly for its Lord; he could come at any hour. In the Jewish community it is a custom on the night of the Passover to send a child to the door to see whether Elijah is already standing outside waiting.

Hebrews 4:1-11

Estomihi

I

Our text belongs to the section beginning at 3:7 and ending at 4:13, and this section unfolds the actual theme of the entire epistle: the pilgrim status of the people of God. The epistle moves along altogether in the style of a sermon, "the earliest independent primitive Christian sermon that has been preserved for us" (Michel). The internal situation in the community to which this sermon is addressed is fairly clear: struggle and great strain on its faith now lie behind it; at present the community has been seized by weariness and slackness, a "creeping debilitation of the inner life" (Schlatter). Above all, its "confession of hope" (10:23) has become atrophied. Our text is concerned also with this malady.

II

First some details: The "now" in verse 1 is an important "therefore" (the subject is those who have not reached the goal set for them by God). Even over the Christian life there hangs the danger of "staying behind" in their pilgrimage. The text of verse 2b has variant traditions. The preferable reading is the one underlying Luther's translation (though in a somewhat shorter version): "because it [the word] was not united with the hearers by faith," that is, it was indeed heard, but heard without faith. Calvin speaks here of a faith which without the heard word is nothing. But it is also true that without faith the word is of no avail. Schlatter prefers another reading: "because they did not unite in faith with those who had heard it" (thus *synkekarasmenous*). Israel has detached herself from Moses and the other great messengers of God—thus the danger of neglect of the primary witnesses! The proclamation of "rest" is based exclusively on God's words and not on any human longing or anything else. In fact, the idea is this: God has promised Israel rest; but since this promise to Israel has not been entirely fulfilled—even Joshua did not bring Israel to complete rest—that rest is yet to be gained (vs. 9). Behind this line of argument there is that insistence, so foreign to our way of thinking but in the Old Testament so vigorously and stubbornly maintained, about the word of God once it is spoken. A word of God once given can be delayed, and it can become necessary for this word to be repeated over a period of time, but it can never fail; for in contrast to every word of man, it is no "empty word" (rek). Instead, it has creative power, and under any and all circumstances it will come to fulfillment (Deut. 32:47; Isa. 55:10ff.). For this reason verses 12-13 in this chapter stand in the very closest connection with our text. In dividing the material into pericopes those verses were separated from this passage because even by themselves they contain abundant material for a sermon.

What is said about rest in our text is taken by the author from the Old Testament, and thus it combines two entirely different and independent traditions. In the case of the Deuteronomic theology, "rest from all enemies round about" was the blessing of salvation toward which Israel was set in motion (Deut. 12:9-10; 25:19). Here and elsewhere this menuchah is understood as a historical and immanent blessing of salvation of a political entity, a people, and the Deuteronomistic way of writing history perceived it as already actualized in part in individual epochs in history (Josh. 21:43ff.; I Kings 8:56). But if one considers the fact that Deuteronomy is a comparatively late theological sketch and that its promises were still being pronounced over the Israel of King Josiah, one can see that even that late era was regarded as still standing between promise and final fulfillment. The promised rest obviously was understood in a much more spiritual sense, for Psalm 95:11, where the motif is sounded again, speaks of God's rest into which it was promised Israel should enter. Now this brings us very close to the second quotation cited in our context, namely that of the protological rest of God (Gen. 2:1ff.). The priestly creation narrative concludes with a reference to God's resting. But this rest is by no means solely a matter that concerns God; instead it is, like God's creative work, a gift of God to the world. When God blesses this rest, it is, so to speak, a third entity between God and the world. To be sure, at first this rest is entirely without reference to man; only when a people of Israel was at hand was its life mysteriously bound up with this rest of God (Exod. 31:12ff.). But God had already prepared this rest from the very beginning; with it he "completed" the world on the seventh day not on the sixth (Gen. 2:2)! Thus he intended the world for this rest. In these two Old Testament

122

witnesses the book of Hebrews sees portrayed the content of the heavenly blessings toward which the Christian people of God are moving: "a definition of the perpetual sabbath in which the sum of human blessedness consists" (Calvin). Calvin clearly perceives that the Old Testament (Deuteronomic) promise of rest is not speaking of a heavenly blessing; but Canaan is "image and symbol of a spiritual heritage;" the rest that is promised to Israel is a foreshadowing. Elsewhere the book of Hebrews characterizes the heavenly consummation as dwelling in a city (11:10; 13:14).

III

About preaching on this text: The two focal points of pilgrim status and rest are thematically given for every sermon on this text, and every such sermon must hold to them in some fashion. But a great deal depends on how this is done. Our text is a favorite for reading in services of the absolution of the dead or at gravesides. But one must guard against a one-sided utilization of this text, for the assertion that Christians are God's pilgrim people is a very realistic affirmation. It is not a statement that is pertinent only at the end of life; instead, it pertains also and all the more so to the youth, and indeed to those who are just entering upon life and beginning a reflective existence. The tone of the entire text, in fact, is much more that of warning than of comfort. This rest is not at all to be evaluated in terms of a contrast with attitudes of weariness and pessimistic outlook on life. The impression that "everything is transient and is slipping away" (Hofmannsthal) is a possibility for all men—as a universal experience; and it is far from coinciding exactly with the experiences of the pilgrim people of God. Nor is there any more possibility of establishing a connection of this sense with the basic attitude of resignation manifested by the existentialists. A look at these latter, and at others, can make us aware that the experience of being on the move, as the book of Hebrews sees it, is not a universal and philosophical truth. We are under way because Christ calls us to a way "whose goal he shows us in promise, one whose goal can be reached only in association with him and his promise" (Käsemann). The great difference is, however, that melancholy looks backward, while our text summons us to look forward. Thus Christ and his word are the real causes of the Christians' restlessness and pilgrimage. Christ commands us again and again to break camp and move on. How many regions of the mind and spirit has Christianity wandered through; and how many shelters that it has built to make some small provision for itself—whether in the political and ideological realm or in philosophical systems or in the realm of esthetics—have been demolished. But God is also constantly leading the individual out of and beyond what he has arbitrarily regarded as his home. Although the text does not afford a specific point of support for doing so, yet it demands of the preacher that he also say a word about that rest that Jesus bestows even in this life (Matt. 11:29 but also Mark 4:39). Indeed, something may be said about Sunday, for in every single week God inserts into our everyday life a sign that points to what is ultimate—God's new world. The unique analogy to the Christian existence that consists of this action of being drawn by God and his word into a pilgrimage is offered by Old Testament Israel, particularly by that puzzling interim of the wilderness-wandering between the reception of the promise and its fulfillment, before the entrance into the rest of the Promised Land. The story of water supplied from miraculous springs, of wars, of being fed by manna, of the gifts of the leaders, of the advance scouts, these provide an inexhaustible supply of portrayals of all the assaults and consolations experienced by the pilgrim people of God who are the Christians! Here of course our text was intended, somewhat one-sidedly, as a warning; that is shown by the very first words of our text, the admonition to fear (vs. 1). The theological impact of that exhortation certainly is somewhat unsettling, but it should not have been replaced in our Luther translations by a much less forceful translation (in the September Bible and all the revised editions of Luther's translation it reads "hence let us now fear"). Schlatter (in his *Erläuterungen*) strives to clarify the relationship of faith to fear: the fear that is meant does not consist in our not daring wholly to place our trust in the gospel; instead, "we fear our unbelief." This is also a serious and important theme for a Christianity that is bathed in blessedness and grace. In the face of all this the sermon on our text should calmly treat of fear in the context of our pilgrimage. Israel knew what was the real cause for distress in the pilgrimage; it lay in the fact that with his people God himself had not yet reached his rest. David was troubled by this (Ps. 132:3-5), and Solomon prayed "And now arise, O Lord God, and go to thy resting place, thou and the ark of thy might" (II Chron. 6:41 RSV). Thus also with us, with our patterns of thought, and so on, Christ has not yet come to his rest—the changes in Christology bear witness to this!—and fear resides in all that we say. The note that is sounded in several expositions is correct: according to the view expressed in this epistle the people of God will surely reach the goal; it is only the individual, the "anyone" of verse 11, that is in danger. The sermon should be addressed to that "anyone" and should exhort him, wherever he may take up residence, to keep his windows open toward Jerusalem (Dan. 6:10).